First World War
and Army of Occupation
War Diary
France, Belgium and Germany

23 DIVISION
Divisional Troops
128 Field Company Royal Engineers
31 August 1915 - 31 October 1917

WO95/2177/3

The Naval & Military Press Ltd
www.nmarchive.com
Published in association with The National Archives

Published by

The Naval & Military Press Ltd

Unit 10 Ridgewood Industrial Park,

Uckfield, East Sussex,

TN22 5QE England

Tel: +44 (0) 1825 749494

www.naval-military-press.com

www.nmarchive.com

This diary has been reprinted in facsimile from the original. Any imperfections are inevitably reproduced and the quality may fall short of modern type and cartographic standards.

© **Crown Copyright**
Images reproduced by permission of The National Archives, London, England, 2015.

Contents

Document type	Place/Title	Date From	Date To
Heading	WO95/2177/3		
Heading	23rd Division 128th Field Coy R.E. Aug 1915-1917 Oct To Italy		
War Diary	Bertham	31/08/1915	11/09/1915
War Diary	Erquinghem	12/09/1915	13/09/1915
War Diary	Rue Marle	14/09/1915	31/10/1915
Heading	23rd Division 128th 7. C. R.E. Vol. 2 Nov 15		
War Diary	Rue Marle Armentieres	01/11/1915	30/11/1915
Heading	23rd Div 128th C.R.E. Vol. 3		
War Diary		01/12/1915	31/12/1915
Heading	23 Div 128th 7 C.R.E. Vol. 4 Jan		
War Diary		01/01/1916	31/01/1916
War Diary	Rue Marle	01/02/1916	14/02/1916
War Diary	Vieux Berquin	15/02/1916	15/02/1916
War Diary	Reserve Area	16/02/1916	23/02/1916
War Diary	Neuf Berquin	24/02/1916	26/02/1916
War Diary	Reserve Area	27/02/1916	29/02/1916
War Diary	Calonne Ricouart	01/03/1916	11/03/1916
War Diary	Villers Au Bois	12/03/1916	18/03/1916
War Diary	Souchez Sector	19/03/1916	30/03/1916
War Diary	Souchez	30/03/1916	31/03/1916
War Diary	Aix-Noulette	01/04/1916	18/05/1916
War Diary	Aix-Noulette Souchez Sector	19/05/1916	11/06/1916
War Diary	Aix-Noulette	12/06/1916	13/06/1916
War Diary	La Thieuloye	14/06/1916	15/06/1916
War Diary	Verchin	16/06/1916	16/06/1916
War Diary	Matringhem	17/06/1916	24/06/1916
War Diary	En Route	25/06/1916	25/06/1916
War Diary	Yzeux	26/06/1916	30/06/1916
Heading	War Diary Of 128th (Field) Company-Royal Engineers From 1st July 1916 to 31st July 1916 (Volume XII).		
War Diary	La Houssoye	01/07/1916	01/07/1916
War Diary	Millen Court	02/07/1916	02/07/1916
War Diary	Albert	03/07/1916	07/07/1916
War Diary	Albert Reference 57d. SE & 62d. NE	08/07/1916	10/07/1916
War Diary	Albert	11/07/1916	12/07/1916
War Diary	Baizieux	13/07/1916	25/07/1916
War Diary	Becourt Wood	26/07/1916	31/07/1916
Operation(al) Order(s)	23rd Division-C.R.E. Order No. S. 8. Appendix I	09/07/1916	09/07/1916
Diagram etc	Sketch Of Strong Point-Vieux Manoir at Contalmaison		
Heading	23rd Divisional Engineers 128th Field Company R.E. August 1916		
Heading	War Diary Of 128th (Field) Company, R.E. From 1st August 1916 To 31st August 1916 (Volume XIII)		
War Diary	Becourt Wood	01/08/1916	07/08/1916
War Diary	Bresle	08/08/1916	14/08/1916
War Diary	Mont des Cats	15/08/1916	17/08/1916
War Diary	Pont de Nieppe	17/08/1916	31/08/1916
Miscellaneous	Reference Fire Trench Completed		
Map	Appendix II		

Heading	War Diary Of 128th (Field) Company RE From 1st September 1916 To 30th September 1916 (Volume XIV)		
War Diary	Pont de Nieppe	01/09/1916	02/09/1916
War Diary	Meteren	03/09/1916	04/09/1916
War Diary	Bleue Maison	05/09/1916	10/09/1916
War Diary	Allonville	11/09/1916	11/09/1916
War Diary	Bresle	12/09/1916	12/09/1916
War Diary	Becourt	13/09/1916	19/09/1916
War Diary	Becourt Wood	18/09/1916	30/09/1916
Miscellaneous	Handing O & S Report 128th Coy RE to 94th Coy RE Appendix I	03/09/1916	03/09/1916
Miscellaneous	List of Maps Landed over to 94th (Fd) Coy RE. by O.C. 128th (Fd) Coy R.E.	03/09/1916	03/09/1916
Miscellaneous	Appendix 2		
Heading	War Diary Of 128th (Field) Company R.E. From 1st October 1916 To 31st October 1916 (Volume XV)		
War Diary	Becourt Wood	01/10/1916	12/10/1916
War Diary	In train	13/10/1916	13/10/1916
War Diary	Coulonvillers	14/10/1916	15/10/1916
War Diary	Poperinghe	16/10/1916	17/10/1916
War Diary	Ypres	18/10/1916	31/10/1916
Miscellaneous	Handing Over Report From 128th (F) Coy RE To 91st (F) Coy RE Appendix I	08/10/1916	08/10/1916
Map			
Heading	War Diary Of 128th (Field) Company R.E. From 1st November 1916 To 30th November 1916 Volume XVI		
War Diary	Ypres	01/11/1916	30/11/1916
Heading	War Diary Of 128th (Field) Company R.E. From 1st December 1916 To 31st December 1916 (Volume XVII)		
War Diary	Ypres	01/12/1916	31/12/1916
War Diary	War Diary Of 128th (Field) Company RE From January 1st 1917 To January 31st 1917. (Volume XVIII)		
War Diary	Ypres	01/01/1917	31/01/1917
Heading	War Diary Of 128th (Field) Company Royal Engineers From 1st February 1917 To 28th February 1917 (Volume XIX)		
War Diary	Ypres	01/02/1917	28/02/1917
Heading	War Diary Of 128th (Field) Company R.E. From 1st March 1917 To 31st March 1917 (Volume XX)		
War Diary	Lederzeele	01/03/1917	01/03/1917
War Diary	Ererlecques	02/03/1917	18/03/1917
War Diary	Broxeele	19/03/1917	19/03/1917
War Diary	Herzeele	20/03/1917	20/03/1917
War Diary	Winnezeele	21/03/1917	31/03/1917
Heading	War Diary Of 128th (Field) Company RE From 1st April 1917 To 30th April 1917 (Volume XXI)		
War Diary	Winnezeele	01/04/1917	07/04/1917
War Diary	Ypres	07/04/1917	30/04/1917
Miscellaneous	Handing Over Report By 227th Field Coy R.E.	15/04/1917	15/04/1917
Miscellaneous	Handing Over Report 234 To 128 Field Coys RE.		
Miscellaneous	CRE 23rd Division. Appendix II	16/04/1917	16/04/1917
Miscellaneous	Oxford St-Al China Wall About 250 Dons To Continued To Gordon Houje Work Going On In 3 Places.		

Heading	War Diary Of 128th Field Company R.E. From 1st May 1917 To 31st May 1917 (Volume XXII)		
War Diary	Ypres	01/05/1917	01/05/1917
War Diary	Steenwoorde	02/05/1917	09/05/1917
War Diary	Ouderdom	10/05/1917	31/05/1917
Heading	War Diary Of 128th Field Company R.E. From 1st June 1917 To 30th June 1917. (Volume XXIII)		
War Diary	Ouderdom	01/06/1917	12/06/1917
War Diary	Zillebeke	13/06/1917	14/06/1917
War Diary	Dickebusch	15/06/1917	22/06/1917
War Diary	Fletre	23/06/1917	28/06/1917
War Diary	Dickebusch	29/06/1917	29/06/1917
War Diary	Spoil Bank	30/06/1917	30/06/1917
Miscellaneous	Headqrs A Herewith War Diary of 128th field Coy R.E. for month of July 14 Please acknowledge	05/06/1914	05/06/1914
Heading	War Diary Of 128th Field Company R.E. 1st July To 31st July 1917 Volume XXIV		
War Diary	Spoil Bank	01/07/1917	02/07/1917
War Diary	Larch Wood	03/07/1917	20/07/1917
War Diary	Dickebush	21/07/1917	29/07/1917
War Diary	X 10.b.6.8. (Fontaine Houck)	30/07/1917	31/07/1917
Heading	War Diary 128th Field Co R.E. Aug 1st-Aug 31st 1917 Vol 23		
War Diary	X 10 b 6.8 (Fontaine Houck)	01/08/1917	05/08/1917
War Diary	Arques	06/08/1917	06/08/1917
War Diary	Haut Loquin	07/08/1917	07/08/1917
War Diary	N. Of Poperinghe-Vlamertinghe-Road 2/G.6.a.5.7	08/08/1917	08/08/1917
War Diary	28/H.10.b.2.5. (Vlamertinghe)	09/08/1917	14/08/1917
War Diary	28/G.6.a.5.7	15/08/1917	25/08/1917
War Diary	Cafe Belge 28/H.30.a.2.9	26/08/1917	31/08/1917
Miscellaneous	Progress Report Of Work Done By 128th Fd Coy R.E. & A Coy 9th South Staffs Since Coming into the Line	26/08/1917	26/08/1917
Heading	128th Field Co. R.E. War Diary For September 1917 Vol. XXVI		
War Diary	Cafe Belge (H.30.a.2.9)	01/09/1917	03/09/1917
War Diary	X.10.c.3.4. (Fontain-Houck)	04/09/1917	10/09/1917
War Diary	X 10 C 3 A (Fontain Hoek)	11/09/1917	12/09/1917
War Diary	Reninghelst.	13/09/1917	13/09/1917
War Diary	Dickebusch	14/09/1917	23/09/1917
War Diary	H.32.d.4.2. (Westoutre)	24/09/1917	30/09/1917
Heading	128th Field Co. R.E. War Diary For October 1917 Vol. XXVII		
War Diary	H.32.d.4.2. (Westoutre)	01/10/1917	10/10/1917
War Diary	H.36 1d1.2	11/10/1917	11/10/1917
War Diary	H.36.c.3.7	12/10/1917	12/10/1917
War Diary	Elzenwalle	13/10/1917	13/10/1917
War Diary	Chateau	13/10/1917	13/10/1917
War Diary	H.36.c.3.7 (Sheet 28)	14/10/1917	21/10/1917
War Diary	Mont Des Cats 27.Q.24.d.8.8	22/10/1917	31/10/1917
Heading	23rd Division 128th 7 C.R.E. Vol I Sep 1 & Oct 15 Jan 19		

W095/21277/3

23RD DIVISION

128TH FIELD COY R.E.
Aug ~~SEP~~ 1915 - ~~JAN 1919~~
1917 OCT

To ITALY

WAR DIARY
or
INTELLIGENCE SUMMARY.
(Erase heading not required.)

128TH FIELD Co.
No. .... Wheel ....
Date ....
ROYAL ENGINEERS

126 - J - Co'y R.E.

Instructions regarding War Diaries and Intelligence Summaries are contained in F. S. Regs., Part II. and the Staff Manual respectively. Title pages will be prepared in manuscript.

Army Form C. 2118.

Place	Date	Hour	Summary of Events and Information	Remarks and references to Appendices
Bertham	31.8.15	13.0	Left Borden 27.8.15 by two trains starting 9.15 AM & 10.15 AM respectively, arrived Southampton at about 6 am. Present of Co with exp. of transport & 42 mares on S.W. Willen. Arrived Havre at 2.30 AM on 28.8.15. Disembarked transport at 7 AM, cleared docks at 2 pm & went to Camp S. Left Havre at 12 noon on 29.8.15 arrived Strowen at 9.10 am & marched out to BERTHAM arriving in billets at 5.30 pm.	
			31.8.15 Setting down & section drill.	
	1.9.15	18.30	Divisional exercise pencil 6.45 AM return to billets 1 pm- Pre of G.S. wagon taken (dry, not). Rain heavy in pm-	
	2.9.15	18.0	Section & tactical order drill in am. Heavy rain in pm	
	3.9.15	18.45	Arrived the Rents march today but rain being very prevalent, lectures & tactics & testing in billets. Horses standing in deep mud. Division free to town Rouse. Rain.	
	4.9/15		Route march about 12 miles for dismounted section. Clean harness & reserve horse mounts section. Capt. Aws. (?) Dewey & self went to Arvelline ... defenses ... C.E. 2/C Army.- Pas C.I.-	
	5.9.15		Cleaning up lines & preparing to move.	
	6.9.15		Marched into division billeted at CAMPAGNE for night, received 220 horses straw.	
	7.9.15		Left 8.30 marched to BAILLEUL arriving in billets 6.30.	
	8.9.15		Digging. Latrines etc etc. Took over 101st Pontoon & 102nd Pontoon & wagons & drove ...	
	9.9.15		Training. Well digging etc etc hard work at NIEPPE Forest.	
	10.9.15		2 & 4 Sections marched to Candescure to wire billets to make fascines & hurdles. L Bampfield & Christie visits S ? Armentiers	
	11.9.15		1 & 3 Sections to CAUDESCURE & join 2/4 section	

8353 Wt. W2544/1454 700,000 5/15 D. D. & L. A.D.S.S./Forms/C. 2118.

Army Form C. 2118.

128TH FIELD COY.
No.
Date
ROYAL ENGINEERS

WAR DIARY
or
INTELLIGENCE SUMMARY.
(Erase heading not required.)

Instructions regarding War Diaries and Intelligence Summaries are contained in F.S. Regs., Part II. and the Staff Manual respectively. Title pages will be prepared in manuscript.

Place	Date	Hour	Summary of Events and Information	Remarks and references to Appendices
ERQUINGHEM	12.9.15		Packed Pontoon wagons at 4.30 A.M. arrived at 10.10 A.M. & handed its heads to Cox by 182nd Coy. Was return to take over from 1st Wessex Coy. & next round touches with O.C. on which received orders to take over from 17th F. Coy.	
	13.9.15		Went round touches with O.C. 17th F. Coy. & commence taking over. Company at once commenced fatigues. No.1 Section to trenches at 6.30 p.m.	
RUE MAPLE	14.9.15		Took over from O.C. 17th F. Coy. hand its 17th Co. Billets in RUE MAPLE at 8.30 A.M.	
"	15.9.15		Reported to Brigade at 9 A.M. and took instructions for work necessary. Recon. visited trenches & various Wire also acquainted with geography of section. Men on fatigues & working in yard. No.1 Section 200 Sandbags on Wellington Avenue making trench. Coms. trench. No.2 in and 400 " on Breastwork in Estaminet at 7.30 P.M. - 3 Pontoon wagon loads of builders Materials up to Estaminet. Working parties worked on Breastwork Aux. and Wellington Ave. ties 2 A.M. 27. Sandbags firing slit by sniper at 1 A.M. Arrived to firmed at 7.30 had to postpone on account of sniping. Day work. No.4 section in Railway & dugouts. 2 Craters + firing for loads. No.3 working in yard on Floor boards + ratines. No.2 & 3 on night fatigues in Peronne Ave. to Trench surfaces in Wellington	
"	16.9.15		Day 1 section + 290 infantry draining Ration Railway Avenue. 1 section working Wellington Ave. 6. 1 section + 400 infantry on Crutchy Avenue. 1 section + 200 inf. on Wellington Ave. On softener - 1 infantry 1 unwounded not arriving.	
"	17.9.15			
"	18.9.15		No infantry fatigues available. RE's chained planks Railway Ave. - Work a head Rest at Big farm in LILLE road. Night work moving Estam to Corigate Avenue. Pioneers joining Poincke Street to Corigate Avenue	

2353 Wt. W2544/1454 700,000 5/15 D.D.&L. A.D.S.S./Forms/C. 2118.

WAR DIARY
or
INTELLIGENCE SUMMARY.
(Erase heading not required.)

Army Form C. 2118.

Instructions regarding War Diaries and Intelligence Summaries are contained in F. S. Regs., Part II. and the Staff Manual respectively. Title pages will be prepared in manuscript.

Place	Date	Hour	Summary of Events and Information	Remarks and references to Appendices
	19.9.15		Day work 1 section on LILLE Rd. Revetting back for hour way on front line and in front COWGATE Avenue + Minielip Traverses. Night 2 sections + 600 infantry on WELLINGTON and BREASTWORK AVES.	
	20.9.15		Day work. §1 section on LILLE Road held. " " + 100 wf̊s on COWGATE AVE Night " §1 " + 300 " " BREASTWORK AVE. " §1 " + 160 " " COWGATE AVE. Supplies sent to advanced depot. Pioneers on extension of BRICK STREET. One officer + 9 men aiding infantry at LAFLEURIE Rd of Brigade. drawing by civilian party by day.	
	21.9.15		No day working parts except civilian drawing parts. Night 1 section constructing tops trench on COWGATE. whatever at front of COWGATE. 1 section + 150 wf̊s on work 65 yards + left flank. 1 section at LA FLEURIE Rd of Brigade. Pioneers on extension of BRICK ST. + Brick Shut.	
	22.9.15		1 section Working by day. Night- Infantry on COWGATE AVE building + attending to parados in Cft Section. Working parts generally keep THORN AVE SETS on left Bank generally making communication trigon	

WAR DIARY
or
INTELLIGENCE SUMMARY.
(Erase heading not required.)

Army Form C. 2118.

Place	Date	Hour	Summary of Events and Information	Remarks and references to Appendices
RUE MAPLE	23.9.15		Roofing shelters for drivers, laying out standings for horses, repairing fortress in COWGATE AVE. Night. Left flank breastwork continued (250 infantry) Head of COWGATE entrenchment continued. Communication trench at THORN STREET continued. No infantry party reported for this work. Sent up 2 rockets at 8 p.m. for signal for demonstration.	
	24.9.15		Day. Laying down standings for horses & general fatigues. Night. Head up to advance state continuing Breastwork at head of COWGATE AVE and parados in 65. Communication trench behind THORN ST.	
	25.9.15		Went up to Poiriers Advanced H.Q. at 3.30 A.M. Bombardment of enemy trenches at 4.25 A.m. feint attack; standing by all day for orders. Night. Breastwork at head of COWGATE AVE. Constructing parados & traverses in 65 trench, constructing parados behind brigade dug out.	
	26.9.15		Day. General fatigues. No work in trenches. Night. Parados & traverses 65. 14 & repairing front line parapet our divisn. 62 - 63. No infantry. Pioneers on COWGATE AVE.	
	27.9.15		Day. Woke on dug out concreting sides & floor. Constructing dug out at Bde H.Qrs. Night. 400 infantry Breastwork AVE. WILLOW AVE S ein parapet.	
	28.9.15		Day - Building Bomb proof at Bde HQrs, making standings for horses, concreting Bomb proofs in trench 6 near. Night. 300 infantry & pioneers on BREASTWORK AVE - 270 dft B18 rton on WILLOW AVE continuation of THORN STREET.	

WAR DIARY
or
INTELLIGENCE SUMMARY.
(Erase heading not required.)

Place	Date	Hour	Summary of Events and Information	Remarks and references to Appendices
Rue Marle	29.9.15		1 section 25 Inf. + 1 platoon pioneers on tomb proofs and firing steps. 1 section on loose standings and Brigade dug outs. all sections went to trenches. Night 200 infantry and 1 section on BREASTWORK AVE. 100 " " " THORN ST.	
	30.9.15		Day. 1 section RE + 2 platoon Pioneers on Bomb proofs in firing line. 1 " " " Dug outs for Brigade H.Q's + advance H.Q's. Night. 2 " + party working parties 2 section R.E. on RUE DU BOIS Firing parapet. –	
	1.10.15		Day. 1 section R.E. and 2 section Pioneers covering dug outs in front lines. 1 section R.E. on Brigadier dug out and advance dug out and Hone standings. Night. 200 Infantry on BREASTWORK AVENUE. 2 sections R.E. on left flank of relaxchment at RUE DU BOIS.	
	2.10.15		Day. occurs as yesterday. Night. Same as yesterday.	
	3.10.15		Day. Changing from night to day 2 sections in day work. Night. 1 section R.E + 1 platoon pioneers on left flank defence + top of COWGATE AVENUE. – 1 section R.E firing up hurdle revetment at WELLINGTON AVENUE. 1 platoon Pioneers improving parapet of COWGATE AVENUE.	

WAR DIARY or INTELLIGENCE SUMMARY

(Erase heading not required.)

Place	Date	Hour	Summary of Events and Information	Remarks and references to Appendices
	4.10.15.		1 section R.E. & 2 sections Pioneers Bomb proofs in firing line. 1 section R.E. & 30 infantry Brigade Dug out & stairway to same. 30 infantry & party R.E. on communication trenches, standing & draining. Night. Placing hurdles in left of line & work on WELLINGTON AVE. Infantry working front BREASTWORK AVE.	
	5.10.15.		2 sections R.E. on day work. Support Brigade HQrs + BIEZ FARM. Horse standings and Bomb proofs in firing line, repairing & draining avenues. Night. Flank defence left of line & placing hurdles for revetment in WELLINGTON AVE.	
	6.10.15.		2 sections R.E. on day work. Support R.E. HQrs and BIEZ FARM, horse standings (civilians) and bomb proofs in firing line. Repairing & draining communication trenches RAILWAY, HAYSTACK & BRICK ST. Night. Placing hurdles for revetment in WELLINGTON AVE. Left flank defence. 600 infantry on BREASTWORK AVE.	
	7.10.15		2 sections R.E. day work. Cemented bomb proofs Brigade HQ dug out. BIEZ Farm dug out. Horse standings (civilians) BOIS GRENIER Liv. Shelters (civilians). Repairing & draining communication trenches. Night 2 sections R.E. AVONDALE St revetment. WELLINGTON AVE revetment. 300 2/- banking, 300 2/4 banking breastwork. 400 Inf & banking.	
	8.10.15		Day & night same as yesterday except that there were 300 W. Riding on WELLINGTON and no infantry on BREASTWORK.	

WAR DIARY
or
INTELLIGENCE SUMMARY.

(Erase heading not required.)

Army Form C. 2118.

Instructions regarding War Diaries and Intelligence Summaries are contained in F. S. Regs., Part II, and the Staff Manual respectively. Title pages will be prepared in manuscript.

Place	Date	Hour	Summary of Events and Information	Remarks and references to Appendices
	9.10.15		Repairing & cleaning Communications. Covering Comms. Group. burying Drain lines standings. Providing shuttle in Bois GRENIER Ave. Dug outs at Bois Hd Qrs. 14 BIEZ FARM. Levelling for drainage scheme. Night firing under for revetment of AVONDALE St. 1 section revetting WELLINGTON AVE. Pioneers in COWGATE.	
	10.10.15		No day work changing or time from day to night work. C of E 70 R.C. inspected C of E Service at 11 AM in Wilds. Night : 1 section on AVONDALE AVE 1 section on WELLINGTON AVE. fixing loopholes in front Parapet.	
	11.10.15		Making Gratings in front line. Dug outs at Hd Qr 2 & BIEZ farm. shelters in BOIS GRENIER line t. arm in S of old Ma[?] pump gear at RUE MARLE. House standings - Levelling for S[?] conversion. Planting Down St. Night 1 section RE 1 2 sections Pioneers on Shine covering for [?] RE inspecting pump at HdQr the Bois Pioneers in [?] COWGATE & BRICK ST.	
	12.10.15		Bde Hd Qrs dug out at BIEZ FM. Am't Sh[?] drain in S. his house standings Repairs ASC Road & ca. Breast work in front line trods in S. his house standings Repairs ASC Road & ca. Night water pumps & repair do. Convent Shin. Piman BRICK ST. 1 & 1/2 Percolators. 100 Sale tip 100 Wire.	

WAR DIARY or INTELLIGENCE SUMMARY

Army Form C. 2118.

(Erase heading not required.)

Instructions regarding War Diaries and Intelligence Summaries are contained in F.S. Regs., Part II. and the Staff Manual respectively. Title pages will be prepared in manuscript.

[Stamp: 125TH FIELD COY. ROYAL ENGINEERS]

Place	Date	Hour	Summary of Events and Information	Remarks and references to Appendices
	13.10.15.		Bott. H.Q. Dugout. Draining Bott GRENIER line and construct steam & pln. Bomb proofs in front line. Boarding of line. Horse standings. Pipes dump. Construct bomb store. Connect S line to semi-circular (2nd and 3rd). Protect pumps & drains. Pioneers in BRICK ST. — 200 Inf. in BREAST WORK AVE. Night Connect S line to semi-circular (2nd and 3rd). Protect pumps & drains. Pioneers in BRICK ST. — 200 Inf. in BREAST WORK AVE. 100 in SALOP & 100 in WINE ST. —	
	14.10.15.		Same as yesterday.	
	15.10.15.		Day. Same as yesterday. Night. 100 Inf. in SALOP AVE. 50 on WINE ST. 200 on WELLINGTON AVE. 2 Section R.E. & 4 Section Pioneers on conversion of S line — remainder of Pioneers on BRICK ST.	
	16.10.15.		Day. Making Bomb proofs in front line, and Shelters for Inf. Officers. Seeing in new caseme of mine shaft in Salient to convert into well. Draining & boarding communication trenches. Completing Dugouts at Advanced Bde H.Q. & BIEZ farm. Shelters in Bott GRENIER line — Horse standings. Night. Conversion of S line — Pioneers in BRICK ST — 200 Inf. in WELLINGTON AVE.	
	17.10.15.		No day work, changing shifts. Night. Converting S line — Pioneers on BRICK ST.	
	18.10.15.		Day. Constructing Dugouts at Bde. H.Q. BIEZ farm. Bomb shelter in BOIS GRENIER line. Bomb props in front line. Concreting round mine shaft in Salient. Draining & boarding communication trenches. Improve protection for 2 Bott & 1 section of Pioneers provide shelters to traverse Bott GRENIER line.	

WAR DIARY
or
INTELLIGENCE SUMMARY.
(Erase heading not required.)

Army Form C. 2118.

Instructions regarding War Diaries and Intelligence Summaries are contained in F. S. Regs. Part II. and the Staff Manual respectively. Title pages will be prepared in manuscript.

Place	Date	Hour	Summary of Events and Information	Remarks and references to Appendices
	18.10.15.	Night.	100 yds on WINE AVE – 100 on SALOP – 200 BREASTWORK AVE 2 sections RE + working Parties on conversion of S. line. Remainder of Coy Parties on BRICK St.	
	19.10.15.	Day.	Bomb store on BOIS GRENIER line. Shelters. Traverses &c. Bomb proofs in front line. Drains &c and communication trenches standings.	
		Night 75 yds	on WINE AVE – 75 on SALOP. – 2 sections RE + 4 sections Pioneers on conversion of S. line. – Pioneers on BRICK St.	
	20.10.15	Day.	Bomb proofs in front line. Drains &c making communication trenches + providing shelters in BOIS GRENIER line – Horse standings.	
	"	Night.	No infantry working parties – 2 sections RE + Pioneers on conversion of S. line. Loopholing parapet. Pioneers on BRICK St.	
	21.10.15	Day.	Bomb proofs in front line. Shelters for officers &c. Traversing + providing shelters in BOIS GRENIER line. Horse standings.	
		Night.	200 yds " on WELLINGTON AVE. 70 on BREASTWORK. 30 on HQrs Dugout + carrying parties – Conversion of S. line.	
	22.10.15	Day.	Repair BOIS GRENIER line. Provide trench boards and shelters in front line. Infantry + training communications.	
		Night.	Conversion of S line + work on BRICK St – 300 yds on WELLINGTON AVE. 200 on WINE St + GOC's dug out.	
	23.10.15	Day.	B.P.S in front line. Reinforcements to Infantry attachment of Sabine. Clean out ARTILLERY Road. Engineer Communications + BOIS GRENIER line.	
		Night.	Digging area by trenching party east of NAIROBI + BLANTYRE Roads	

WAR DIARY
or
INTELLIGENCE SUMMARY.
(Erase heading not required.)

Army Form C. 2118.

Instructions regarding War Diaries and Intelligence Summaries are contained in F. S. Regs., Part II. and the Staff Manual respectively. Title pages will be prepared in manuscript.

[Stamp: 128TH FIELD CO — No. Shed 10 — ROYAL ENGINEERS]

Place	Date	Hour	Summary of Events and Information	Remarks and references to Appendices
	23.10.15		Relieve 6th Bn of posts	
	24.10.15		Changing shifts. Laying out assembly trenches.	
			Night:– Digging assembly trenches.	
	25.10.15		Day:– PPS in front line. Providing recesses for cylinders in salient & Little Salient. Laying out approaches & making bridges for same.	
			Night: 300 hp 4 RE & Pioneers digging assembly trenches.	
	26.10.15		Day:– Providing recesses in parapet – constructing gun emplt. knife rests. Carrying from dumps of Communication trenches with wire netting.	
			Night: Digging assembly trenches.	
	27.10.15		Day:– Providing recesses in parapet. 1st Cav. Div. building emplacements. C.O.2 on Communications. (Rain)	
			Night: 100 Inf.try on WELLINGTON AVE. so covering 13th JKO's dug out.– 50 on New Bath HD's @ Rear ARTILLERY ROAD.	
28.10.15.			Provide recesses in parapet. Road & drain communication trenches. (Rain)	
			Night: New Bath HD's Rear ARTILLERY ROAD. 3 officers.	
29.10.15.			Providing & repair parapets (coming down with the rain) RE provide recesses in parapet. Repair 3 lines.	
	30.10.15.		Night: New Bath HD's Rear Artillery Road.	
			Provide recesses in parapet. Rep'r parapets, revetments, slip ways. Repair 3 lines. Support.	

WAR DIARY
or
INTELLIGENCE SUMMARY.

Army Form C. 2118.

Place	Date	Hour	Summary of Events and Information	Remarks and references to Appendices
	30.10.15	Night	Near Bnt.a No 2. Repair ditch along Rue du Bois. Sapping.	
	31.10.15		No day work. Changing shifts. Rain.	
		Night	Near Bnt.a No 2 - Repair B.a No 2 at Orchard. Repair AID post on Moystaten. Sealed light sumps. Deepen ditch in R. du Bois	

JSnelson
Major R.E.
O.C. 128TH FIELD COY. R.E.

128ᵗʰ F.C. R.E.
Vol: 2

121/7693

23ʳᵈ Hussein(?)

Nov 15.

Instructions regarding War Diaries and Intelligence Summaries are contained in F. S. Regs., Part II. and the Staff Manual respectively. Title pages will be prepared in manuscript.

Army Form C. 2118.

WAR DIARY
or
INTELLIGENCE SUMMARY.
(Erase heading not required.)

Place	Date	Hour	Summary of Events and Information	Remarks and references to Appendices
RUE MARIE J.M.15 ARMENTIERES	1.11.15	Day	Improve communication in Salient - Put in G.s screens in parapet. Concrete front portes.	
		Night	Work on new B.O.'s J.8.9. - M.G. emplacements in church of Salient - S.L. emp? Repair roof of 100's. Overhead + A.W. Pat HAYSTACK AVE.	
	2.11.15	Day	Concrete B.P.'s. Repair parapets. Practice attack.	
		Night	Work on New B.Os. M.G. emp? in Church - S.L. emp? Repair roof of left Section H.Q. + Aid Post HAYSTACK.	
	3.11.15	Day	Making Dugouts. Repair parapets + sapping.	
		Night	Repair roof HQ's left section + Aid Post HAYSTACK + F.O.O. Post. M.G. emp? in Church. Revet Comm? in Salient.	
	4.11.15	Day	Bull Dam + wheries. Parade. Repair parapets in front line + Supports. H.Q. Co's S. Staffords in Railway AVE.	
		Night	Repair roof H.Q's left section + Aid Post HAYSTACK. S.L. emp? Repair M.G. emp? in Salient. Improve SALOR AVE. Repair parapet on bridge between 62-63 Comd.	
	5.11.15	Day	Repair parapets in 66 rains foot bomb's in WINE AVE. repair parapets + traverses. Pienies in RAILWAY AVE.	
		Night	Completed roofing HQ's left Section. Continue roof of Aid Post. Putting in aprons in Support line. Revetting. Put revetments in Salient.	

WAR DIARY
or
INTELLIGENCE SUMMARY.
(Erase heading not required.)

Instructions regarding War Diaries and Intelligence Summaries are contained in F. S. Regs., Part II. and the Staff Manual respectively. Title pages will be prepared in manuscript.

Army Form C. 2118

128TH FIELD COY
No. ....
Date May 1915
ROYAL ENGINEERS

Place	Date	Hour	Summary of Events and Information	Remarks and references to Appendices
	6.11.15	Day	Repair parapets. Work on HAYSTACK & RAILWAY Guns.	
		Night	Repair of A1A pvt. Removed entanglement to Solient, put entanglers in S. line & AVONDALE.	
	7.11.15	Day	No work during shifts - Church parade.	
		Night	Conversion of S. line to Semi trestwork. Revet trench to Solient trench AVONDALE read for revetment.	
	8.11.15	Day	Repair parapets & communications. Work on S. line.	
		Night	Conversion of S. line. Build bridge at BIEZ farm. Revet AVONDALE Rd.	
	9.11.15	Day	Prepare AVONDALE. Work on S. line & in Solient.	
		Night	Cement S. line & revet AVONDALE.	
	10.11.15	Day	Revet AVONDALE. Work on S. line & draining.	
		Night	Cement S. line. Revet AVONDALE. Improve RUE du BOIS.	
	11.11.15	Day	Provided stores for informing WINE St. & fortress d. Repair first parapet & shore up shelters.	
		Night	Put in anchors in WINE St. AVONDALE. Cement S. line & screw RUE du BOIS	
	12.11.15	Day	Work on WINE St. S. line AVONDALE & Repair parapets	
		Night	Cement S. line. Put in anchors in WINE St. AVONDALE & put up cement barrels for use as latrines	

WAR DIARY
or
INTELLIGENCE SUMMARY.
(Erase heading not required.)

Army Form C. 2118.

128TH FIELD COY.
No. ....
Date Nov 1915
ROYAL ENGINEERS

Instructions regarding War Diaries and Intelligence Summaries are contained in F. S. Regs., Part II. and the Staff Manual respectively. Title pages will be prepared in manuscript.

Place	Date	Hour	Summary of Events and Information	Remarks and references to Appendices
	13.11.15	Day	WINE AVE. Thicken parapet in ORCHARD & new Rd. Avondale St front line. Wire in S. line. Improve Griernes parapet. Draining.	
		Night	Count S line. Anchors in AVONDALE - WINE AVE. Improve parapet in HAYSTACK	
	14.11.15	Day	Clamps & lifts. Church. Count S line. Anchors in AVONDALE - Erect Screen on LILLE ROAD. Serve RUE du BOIS. Improve parapet HAYSTACK.	
	15.11.15	Day	Count S line. Revet clamps of Salient. Revet & clamp WINE AVE. Repair Stilletos in front line. Draining.	
		Night	Count S line. Anchors in AVONDALE & WINE ST. Improve parapet on S.S. line between HAYSTACK & WINE AVES.	
	16.11.15	Day	Repair revetment to Salient. Improve comt. between orchard & HAYSTACK. Improve upper sap of Salient. Count S line. Work on WINE ST. Drainage. new GATE.	
		Night	Count S line. Anchors in HAYSTACK & AVONDALE & WINE ST.	
	17.11.15	Day	S line - Removal Clamps of Salient. Protect pumps. Improve revetment of 66 & Stilletos in 66. Revet AVONDALE. Rain stopped work in QUEEN ST. Draining.	
		Night	Count S line. Anchors in AVONDALE & revetment to Salient + WINE ST.	

WAR DIARY
or
INTELLIGENCE SUMMARY.
(Erase heading not required.)

Instructions regarding War Diaries and Intelligence Summaries are contained in F.S. Regs., Part II. and the Staff Manual respectively. Title pages will be prepared in manuscript.

Army Form C. 2118.

108TH FIELD COY.
No. ....
Date. Nov 1915
ROYAL ENGINEERS

Place	Date	Hour	Summary of Events and Information	Remarks and references to Appendices
	18.11.15	Day	Revised Chnd to Salient & erect shelters. Rain flow of QUEEN ST. work in AVONDALE & Shin - Drainage	
		Night	Conveyed Shin anchors in AVONDALE + Chnd of Salient.	
	19.11.15	Day	Work on WINE St. COWGATE. Shin Chnd of Salient AVONDALE - 66	
		Night	Conveyed Shin anchors in AVONDALE + Chnd of Salient + WINE St.	
	20.11.15	Day	S. Liu. Chnd of Salient. AVONDALE - Revetment to 66 - WINE St COWGATE + chaining	
		Night	Same as last night.	
	21.11.15	Day	No work. Church.	
		Night	Same as last night.	
	22.11.15	Day	Revised Chnd of Salient + revetment of 66 - S.Liu - WINE ST COWGATE + draining	
		Night	Same as last night.	
	23.11.15	Day	Same as yesterday	
		Night	Same as yesterday	
	24.11.15	Day	4 sections all on Coy work on account of relief of Brigade (with same work as yesterday)	
	25.11.15	Day	Conveyed Shin under Chnd of Salient, in from AVONDALE, revet COURANT du Le Chapelle in front QUEEN ST - WINE AVE - HAY STACK + COWGATE, draining	

(123TH FIELD COY. Army Form C. 2118
No...... Nov 1915
ROYAL ENGINEERS)

WAR DIARY
or
INTELLIGENCE SUMMARY.
(Erase heading not required.)

Instructions regarding War Diaries and Intelligence Summaries are contained in F. S. Regs., Part II. and the Staff Manual respectively. Title pages will be prepared in manuscript.

Place	Date	Hour	Summary of Events and Information	Remarks and references to Appendices
	25.11.15	night	Convent S.trin. trailers in AVONDALE & Chord of SALIENT + WINE AVE	
	26.11.15	Day	S.trin. QUEEN ST. AVONDALE. WINE AVE. COWGATE & HAYSTACK. Underpinning front parapet. Erect new accommodation H.Q2 at ORCHARD 9 Convent.	
		Night	Same as yesterday.	
	27.11.15	Day	Same as yesterday.	
		Night	Same as yesterday.	
	28.11.15	Day	Chords + Shifts. Church	
		Night	S.trin. Carrying. tradings in AVONDALE - WINE ST. + repair parapet I21.u.6 found extra accommodation HQ2 in field of AVONDALE RE Draining + revetting Convent.	
	29.11.15	Day	S.trin - Chord of Salient.	
		Night	No night work. M.G's working.	
	30.11.15	Day	S.trin - Chord of Salient. AVONDALE RE revet Convent draining.	
		Night	S.trin Carrying in. Revet AVONDALE - provide extra accommodation at ORCHARD.	

J Bowen
Major RE
O.C. 123rd F. Coy RE

23rd Div

128th F.C.R.E.
Vol: 3

121
7909

128TH FIELD COY.
ROYAL ENGINEERS

WAR DIARY
or
INTELLIGENCE SUMMARY.
(Erase heading not required.)

Instructions regarding War Diaries and Intelligence Summaries are contained in F. S. Regs., Part II. and the Staff Manual respectively. Title pages will be prepared in manuscript.

Place	Date	Hour	Summary of Events and Information	Remarks and references to Appendices
	1.XII.15	Day	Conversion of S hine, and Avondale Road. Revetment of Chevry Salient, and Wins Avenue. Draining no Pioneers work party to relieve	
		Night	Conversion of S hine & Avondale Road, Resting, Whole shelli at Orchard. Draining S hine.	
	2.XII.15	Day	Conversion of S hine & Avondale Road. Repairs to chord of Salient. Revetting Wins Avenue. Draining	O.C. gone on leave
		Night	Conversion of S hine & Avondale Road. Erecting whole shellis in Orchard. Draining S hine. Revetting Wins Avenue.	
	3.XII.15	Day	Conversion of S hine and Avondale Road. Revetment Chord of Salient and Wins Avenue. Draining	
		Night	Conversion of S hine and Avondale Road. Erecting whole shellis in Orchard. Draining S hine. Revetment of Wins Avenue. Repairing Tramline	
	4.XII.15	Day	Conversion of S hine and Avondale Road. Repairs to chord of Salient. Revetment of Wins Avenue. Draining	
		Night	Conversion of S hine and Avondale Road. Whole shellis in Orchard. Draining S hine.	
	5.XII.15	Day	Work No. changed slightly. Coy parade at Divisional Baths	
		Night	Conversion of S hine & Avondale Road. Revetment of Wins Avenue.	
	6.XII.15	Day	Conversion of S hine & Avondale Road. Repairs to chord of Salient. Repairing & draining Upper Wins St. Underpinning dugouts in parapet. Draining. Revetting Banks of Communication	
		Night	Conversion of S hine & Avondale Road. Repairs to Salient. Avenue. Revetment of S hine. No infantry parties in evening but Battalion relief	
	7.XII.15	Day	Conversion of S hine & Avondale Road. Revetting Salient & banks of Communication. General draining. Revetting Wins Avenue.	
		Night	Conversion of S hine & Avondale Road. Digging drain from S hine. Shell collector & cap relief.	
	8.XII.15	Day	Conversion of S hine & Avondale Road. Revetting in Salient, in banks of Communication. Revetting Wins Avenue.	69329 2nd Cpl. MACDONALD E. wounded on S hine
		Night	Pioneer A Coy. Relieved. Parapet Drained. Huts	
			Conversion of S hine & Avondale Road.	
	9.XII.15	Day	Conversion of S hine & Avondale Road. Repairs to Salient & Park Row. Revetting Wins Avenue & banks of Communication. General Draining	
		Night	Conversion of S hine. Claying SALOP Street	

WAR DIARY
or
INTELLIGENCE SUMMARY.
(Erase heading not required.)

Instructions regarding War Diaries and Intelligence Summaries are contained in F. S. Regs., Part II. and the Staff Manual respectively. Title pages will be prepared in manuscript.

Place	Date	Hour	Summary of Events and Information	Remarks and references to Appendices
	10.12.15	Day	Creation of Shin. AVONDALE ROAD. Revetting WINE AVENUE & banks of COURANT. Repairing PARK ROW. Undermining shelter in front parapet. Revetting salient at dusk.	2 Cpls McDONALD & PURVES killed & funeral
	11.12.15	Night	Nil. (Relief)	
		Day	4 section R.E. into a Shin. AVONDALE - WINE Stut - Revetting COURANT Front parapet shelter. Revetting & draining PARK ROW. No one on night work owing to bad weather conditions & detail of firing service output also to large percentage of sick also men in G night work.	
	12.12.15		Support line. AVONDALE - WINE Stut - draining.	
	13.12.15		Communication Shin - AVONDALE - WINE Stut - undermining front parapet. Revetting PARK ROW. Draining. Revetting LONDON BRIDGE & arching.	
	14.12.15		Company at Divisional Baths. Work on STONE LINE and deep cuts to Night work on LONDON Bridge & arching.	
	15.12.15		Communication of Shin. AVONDALE ROAD. WINE Stut. underpinning front parapet. Revetting PARK ROW and draining. 100 Left working with RE Purves on WINE Stut revetting, draining & COW GATE d.o. Night. 12 RE and 50 Inf. driving piles in dry front parapet to support same when digging for S. emplacement - 25 Inf. on new drain - work on LONDON BRIDGE & arching.	
	16.12.15		RE and 100 Inf. big trenches for emplacements in front parapet - Shin - AVONDALE - WINE Stut - PARK ROW draining. Purves on WINE Stut & COW GATE. Night driving piles in front parapet 100 Inf. on parapet AVONDALE. 100 digging in parapet Shin.	
	17.12.15		RE + 150 Inf. Firm groove for emplacements - Shin - AVONDALE ROAD - Revetting SALIENT - WINE Stut - PARK ROW. Draining. Purves on WINE Stut - COW GATE - SALOR.	

WAR DIARY
or
INTELLIGENCE SUMMARY.
(Erase heading not required.)

Instructions regarding War Diaries and Intelligence Summaries are contained in F.S. Regs., Part II and the Staff Manual respectively. Title pages will be prepared in manuscript.

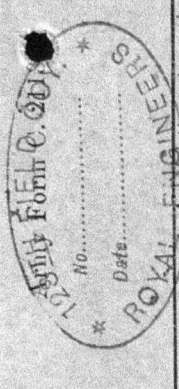

Army Form C. 2118.
No.............
Date............
ROYAL ENGINEERS

Place	Date	Hour	Summary of Events and Information	Remarks and references to Appendices
	17.xii.15	Night	Building parapet on LONDON BRIDGE - Dump piles for emplacements in S. line - Pioneers archiving in SALOP.	
	18.xii.15		RE. (100 Infantry tie irons) - S. line - PATRN Rows. Pioneers hacking Aid post in PARN Row - turts on parados in Salient - MONDALE. Fixing loopes emplacements in parapet - Draining - Pioneers - Wine St - COWGATE revet + chain. Night archiving.	
	19.xii.15		2 Sections RE and 100 infantry. S. line - L. steely boxes in first line. Aid post PATRN Row. - Pioneers not working. Night 100 Inf. in parapet of S. line - RE archiving.	
	20.xii.15		RE and 100 Inf. S. line - loopes in first line - improving parados in Salient. SALOP AVENUE - WINE St. - revetic COURANT cleaning. Pioneers - Wine Avenue - cepair COWGATE - S. line - SALOP. Night 100 Infantry on parapet of S. line. RE driving piles in front parapet + archiving.	
	21.xii.15		RE + 100 Inf. S. line - Salient parados + shelters. Put in loopes + holes in parapet in 10 bays of first line - Revet + chain PARN Row. Resustal Aid Post PATRN Row. cleaning. Pioneers... WINE St. COWGATE revet and sweep.	
	22.xii.15		RE + (100 Inf. tie iron) - S. line - WINE St. Aid post loopes in front parapet. Work in SALIENT - draining + frampring. Pioneers on WINE AVE + COWGATE. Night archiving.	

WAR DIARY
or
INTELLIGENCE SUMMARY.
(Erase heading not required.)

Instructions regarding War Diaries and Intelligence Summaries are contained in F.S. Regs. Part II. and the Staff Manual respectively. Title pages will be prepared in manuscript.

Place	Date	Hour	Summary of Events and Information	Remarks and references to Appendices
	23.xii.15		RE and 120 Inf.ᵗʳʸ Revetted parados in Salient - S.hine - Sandbagging loopes in front line - Revet + drain PARK ROW - Draining. Pioneers WINE AVE COWGATE + upper SALOP revet and drain. Night anchoring.	Lᵗ Cpl Willows W.K. wounded in front line
	24.xii.15		RE and 100 Inf.ᵗʳʸ S.hine - Pumping and repairing in Upper COWGATE. Work on parados in Salient - Putting in loops in front parapet - repairing PARK ROW - Draining. Pioneers Win AVENUE Lower COWGATE upper SALOP revet + drain - drain S.S. line - Night. Anchoring.	
	25.xii.15		RE + 100 Infantry. Pumping + repairing COWGATE - S.hine - Revetting Salient - Putting in G. emplacements in front line - Draining - revetting PARK ROW - Pioneers WINE St. - Lower COWGATE - Upper SALOP + drain. Had a drive for whole company in huts. Night 200 Inf.ᵗʳʸ on S.line.	
	26.xii.15		Pumping + repairing COWGATE + PARK ROW WINE Street.	
	27.xii.15		150 Inf.ᵗʳʸ by day. Night 100 Infantry on S.line.	
	28.xii.15		RE + 100 Infantry Pioneers Making road in PARK ROW WINE AVE + COWGATE. Work on new AID POST WINE AVE.	

Army Form C. 2118
128TH FIELD COY.
ROYAL ENGINEERS

WAR DIARY
or
INTELLIGENCE SUMMARY.
(Erase heading not required.)

Instructions regarding War Diaries and Intelligence Summaries are contained in F. S. Regs., Part II. and the Staff Manual respectively. Title pages will be prepared in manuscript.

Place	Date	Hour	Summary of Events and Information	Remarks and references to Appendices
	28.XII.15		2 Sect RE + 25 Infantry on Aid Post. G. of Lindens fort with implements.	
	29.XII.15		RE and Pioneers. Shin. Aid Post – SALOP AVENUE and draining (no infantry) Night. Aid post & awaiting parties	
	30.XII.15		RE and 120 Infantry. Shine. Cutting drain from Salient – Aid Post Wine Ave. Draining. Pioneers. Revetting + draining SALOP WINE – PARK ROW – Shin. Night. awaiting	
	31.XII.15		RE and 160 Infantry. Shin – Cross fire Salient – PARK Row – Aid Post – Drain't – Pioneers + 20 Infantry. Shin – Upton Salop – PARK Row – WINE AVENUE – CON GATE. Lieut E.W. RUSE – 69380. Corporal FLEMING. 65753 Sp. Churcher – 68914 Sp. Bowren 69403 Sapper Nowes. Getting up charge of gun cotton at Braowin CAPOELLE ARMENTIERE'S for special work with infantry at 5.30 pm about gun cotton exploded causing death of above and wounding 65831. "Cpl. Bloomfield 46093 Sp. Janner 95007 Sp. Kinsale 46709 Sp. Hull.	

Jhs Rowden
Major RE
O.C. 128. Fd. Coy. RE

WAR DIARY
or
INTELLIGENCE SUMMARY.
(Erase heading not required.)

Form C. 2118.

Instructions regarding War Diaries and Intelligence Summaries are contained in F.S. Regs., Part II. and the Staff Manual respectively. Title pages will be prepared in manuscript.

128TH FIELD Co.
ROYAL ENGINEERS

Place	Date	Hour	Summary of Events and Information	Remarks and references to Appendices
	1.1.16	Night	Clearing debris at G. onward dépôt & work on dug outs. Work on S. line.	
	2.1.16	Night	Work on dug outs. Battn parade t[oda]y. S. line.	
	3.1.16	—	Renewing pontoon from R. bge to bldg — S. line — Clear lin. of SALIENT — drawing.	
		Night	S. line & aid post WINE AVE — LONDON BRIDGE.	
	4.1.16		Clear lin. of SALIENT. S. line. Parapet across railway. Wiring in SALIENT — drawing — WINE AVE & other communicat.	
		Night	Aid Post — S. line — LONDON PEREP. rebuild.	
	5.1.16		S. line — Clear lin — SALIENT front footpath draining. Pioneers on communication.	
		Night	Aid Post — S. line.	
	6.1.16		Clear line — S. line — SALIENT Board & drain 59 Trench. draining.	
		Night	Aid Post — S. line.	
	7.1.16		S. line — Clear line — SALIENT — draining. Pioneers on communic. tr. S. line & SS.lin.	
		Night	Aid Post (no infantry available).	
	8.1.16		S. line — Clear line — SALIENT — draining. Pioneers on communic. tr S. line & SS lin.	
		Night	200 Sqft on parapet of S. line — RE Aid Post — fixing water pump in S. line.	
	9.1.16		Clear line — SALIENT — S. line. draining (50 Sqft) Pioneers on comm'n S. line & foot bd S/L.	
		Night	200 Sqft on parapet of SALIENT. S. line. 170 Sqft in AVONDALE — 30 Sqft in AID POST.	
	10.1.16		RE & 100 Sqft. Clear line of SALIENT. SALIENT. S. line — Draining. Revetting COURANT. Pioneers on comm'n Train & roads. SS. line. Shelters in front line.	

#353   Wt. W3544/1454 700,000 5/15 D.D. & L.   A.D.S.S./Forms/C. 2118.

WAR DIARY
or
INTELLIGENCE SUMMARY.
(Erase heading not required.)

Army Form C. 2118.

Instructions regarding War Diaries and Intelligence Summaries are contained in F. S. Regs., Part II. and the Staff Manual respectively. Title pages will be prepared in manuscript.

[Stamp: 128TH FIELD COMPANY ROYAL ENGINEERS]

Place	Date	Hour	Summary of Events and Information	Remarks and references to Appendices
	10.1.16	night	Aid Post. 140 Sufy¹s on S. line parapet.	
	11.1.16	night	Remodel left entrance to SALIENT and ESTAMINET (rue du bois) - S. line - draining. Pioneers - communications. S. line + S.S. line.	
	12.1.16	night	Aid Post. 160 Sufy¹s on S. line parapet. Remodel left of SALIENT + ESTAMINET - S. line - draining - (contd?) Pioneers. PARK ROW - WINE AVE - EALOP - COWGATE + S.line. Aid Post. - 360 Sufy¹s on S. line parapet.	
	13.1.16	night	S. line. Remodel left entrances to SALIENT + ESTAMINET - Put in fire steps in front line - S. line. Aid Post - floor + revetment of ORCHARD. Cleaning S.S. line COWGATE to AVONDALE. Pioneers on Comm¹s to S.S. line. 350 Sufy¹s on S. line parapet.	
	14.1.16	night	Remodel left entrance to SALIENT + ESTAMINET - S. line - Aid Post - fire steps in front line. Clear S.S. line - draining - Tunnel in front of ORCHARD. Pioneers. Comm¹s - S. line + S.S. line. 350 Sufy¹s on parapet of S. line.	
	15.1.16	night	Left of SALIENT + ESTAMINET - fire steps in front line - clear and drain S.S. line - S. line. - AID POST. - Clearing RUE du BOIS - Draining. Pioneers on comm¹s S. line + S.S. line cleaning. No night work.	
	16.1.16	night	S. line. repair floor boards + drainage. RE - on trench in Pioneers working Parapet of Rue du Bois - S. line.	
	17.1.16		S. line - Left of SALIENT + ESTAMINET - Comm¹s along S. line to rear of BURNT FARM	

#353 Wt. W2544/1454 700,000 5/15 D.D.&L. A.D.S.S./Forms/C.2118.

WAR DIARY
or
INTELLIGENCE SUMMARY.
(Erase heading not required.)

Army Form C. 2118.

128TH FIELD CO/
No. ....
Date Jan/16
ROYAL ENGINEERS

Instructions regarding War Diaries and Intelligence Summaries are contained in F.S. Regs., Part II and the Staff Manual respectively. Title pages will be prepared in manuscript.

Place	Date	Hour	Summary of Events and Information	Remarks and references to Appendices
	17.1.16		Jin Piquet mounted near Rt B" 11th Rgt - Trench in front of ORCHARD the Trench S.S. line near HAYSTACK. Clear S.S line - Draining. Pioneers Coming - 2 hrs on Clear S.S line. 115 Inf'y on Shin + Aid Post.	
	18.1.16	night	S.hin reversed Left of SALIENT - S.S line between COWGATE + AVONDALE also near HAYSTACK - Rounded bend near R'B' H.Q. - Clear + board 2 hrs left of BURNT FARM - Rounded bend in front of ORCHARD - Repair shelter in front line - Draining. Pioneers Coming - S.Line + draining. 170 Inf'y on Shin + Aid Post	
	19.1.16	night	S.hin - Left of SALIENT - S.S line near HAYSTACK - Trench near R"B" H.Q. - Clear + board 2 hrs right of BURNT FARM - Repair shelters in front line - Clear S.S line - (no tanks available) 150 Inf'y on Shin + Aid Post.	
	20.1.16	night	Repair shelters in front line - S.S line near HAYSTACK. Trench in front of ORCHARD S.hin near R"B" H.Q. - S.Lin to right of BURNT FARM. - Rounded left of SALIENT. Clear S.S line between COWGATE + AVONGATE. Pioneers Coming - S.hin + drain. 350 Inf'y on S.hin + parapet.	
	21.1.16	night	S.hin - mended left entrance to SALIENT. Sin steps to front line - S.S line near HAYSTACK to front of ORCHARD. S.Lin to right of BURNT FARM + near R"B" H.Q. - Clear S.S line Pioneers Coming S"s on S.hin.	

WAR DIARY
or
INTELLIGENCE SUMMARY.
(Erase heading not required.)

Army Form C. 2118.

128TH FIELD CO Date Jan. 1/16
ROYAL ENGINEERS

Instructions regarding War Diaries and Intelligence Summaries are contained in F.S. Regs., Part II. and the Staff Manual respectively. Title pages will be prepared in manuscript.

Place	Date	Hour	Summary of Events and Information	Remarks and references to Appendices
	21.1.16	Night	nil.	
	22.1.16		S.Line – Left entrance to SALIENT – two steps in front line – S.S. line near HAYSTACK to front of ORCHARD – S. hive to right of BURNT FARM & near Rt Rd M.G. R2 – Clear S.S. line. Pioneers covering 2 hives.	
		Night	150 Infts in S. line & the Rest	
	23.1.16		Left of SALIENT – S. hive – S. line to centre of BURNT FARM & near Rt C.T. M.G. R3 (Inf'y + Pioneers not working).	
		Night	R.E. clearing drain from PARK ROW to DOG LEG R3.	
	24.1.16		Remade left of SALIENT – S. hive. Two steps in front line – S.S. line near HAYSTACK & ORCHARD – S. hive right of BURNT FARM & near Rt C.T. M.G. R2 – AVONDALE. Pioneers covering 2 hives.	
	25.1.16		R.E. clearing drain from PARK ROW.	
			Remade left of SALIENT. S. hive. two steps in front line. S.S. line near HAYSTACK & ORCHARD – S. hive right of BURNT FARM & Rt R2 M.G. R3. Pioneers Park Covers – S. hive – S.S. line – Drains.	
		Night	220 Infantry in S. hive & 410 Rest. 20 " " in AVONDALE – R.E. covering hides in AVONDALE.	
	26.1.16		S. line – Left of SALIENT – two steps in right of SALIENT. S. hive right of BURNT FARM & right Rd M.G. R2 – S.S. hive near HAYSTACK & ORCHARD – M.G. emplacements. Pioneers covering – S.S. hive – S. line.	
		Night	200 Infts on S. hive – 160 on AVONDALE. R.E. Rue du Bois – erecting bridge Framers.	

WAR DIARY
or
INTELLIGENCE SUMMARY.

(Erase heading not required.)

Army Form C. 2118.

128TH FIELD Co
No.......
Date Jan 16
ROYAL ENGINEERS

Instructions regarding War Diaries and Intelligence Summaries are contained in F. S. Regs., Part II. and the Staff Manual respectively. Title pages will be prepared in manuscript.

Place	Date	Hour	Summary of Events and Information	Remarks and references to Appendices
	27.1.16		Remade left of SALIENT & Prop m/g ESTAMINET - fin steps in SALIENT - 52 + 59 Trenches - S.hin right of BURNT FARM + near R¹R² M¹C¹ - HAYSTACK & in front of ORCHARD - (N. infantry) Pioneers on Comm¹² - S.hin & S.S.hin	
	28.1.16.	Right	160 w.f.i in prospect of S.hin S.hin - Tin steps in front line - S.hin right of BURNT FARM & R²R³ M²C² S.S. Line near HAYSTACK + front of ORCHARD - Prepare site for M.G. in f/g Pennfoot & draining Pioneers on comm¹² S hin + SS hin	
	29.1.16	Right	RE clear Rue du Bois - 160 Drift in S. hin S.hin Right of BURNT FARM - S.S. hin near HAYSTACK + ORCHARD Pioneers Comm¹² S hin + SS hin	
	30.1.16	night	S/E.7 Section 1 BM to 8 am repair + revited parapet right + left of ESTAMINET 100 drft in Brown work. (Parapet s/s blown up by enemy with wire entanglement) No day work	
		night	200 drft in S hin - 240 in S S hin	
	31.1.16		Instruks. /R E. S.hin. Tin steps in SALIENT - S hin mears R²R³ - Revited left of ESTAMINET - SS hin near HAYSTACK + ORCHARD - Clear S hin left of COW GATE	

Js [signature]
O.C. 128" field Coy R.E.

1.2.16

WAR DIARY
or
INTELLIGENCE SUMMARY
(Erase heading not required.)

Army Form C. 2118.

Instructions regarding War Diaries and Intelligence Summaries are contained in F.S. Regs., Part II. and the Staff Manual respectively. Title pages will be prepared in manuscript.

Stamp: 178TH FIELD COY. ROYAL ENGINEERS. Date 17 Feb 1916

Place	Date	Hour	Summary of Events and Information	Remarks and references to Appendices
RUE MARLE	1.11.16	Night	R.E. M.G. Emplacements, Overhead Traverse	
	2.11.16		R.E. Putting Fire steps in Salient. Repairs S.Line near Rt Batt⁰ H.Qrs. Remodelling Parapet & Rt of Estaminet (R. de Bois) Rebuilding S.S.Line in front of Orchard and near Haystack Clearing S.Line to left of Cowgate. Draining. Fitting up 4" Pump.	
		Night	PIONEERS Repairs Park Row, Wine Avenue, Salop. S.Line left of Burnt Farm. 200 Infantry on Parapet of S.Line, 140 on Avondale R⁴ parapet. R.E. Anchoring Parties. M.G. Emplacements.	
	3.11.16	Day	R.E. S.Line, Parapet left of Estaminet; S.Line near Rt Batt⁰ H.Qrs. Fire Steps in Salient: Repair revetment on Rt of Estaminet SS. Line, Parapet at head of Orchard, Fire Steps on left of Frontline. M.G. Emplacement C Drain & Pumps. PIONEERS Park Row, S.Line left of Burnt Farm. Relaying Duckboards behind T.I.S.I. Salops, Avondale Ave.	
		Night	200 Infantry on Parapet in S.Line, 150 Infantry on Parapet of Avondale. R.E. M.G. Emplacements & Anchoring parties.	
	4.11.16	Day	R.E. S.Line Parapet left of Estaminet; S.Line near Rt Batt⁰ H.Qrs. Revetment on left of Estaminet; S.S.Line near Haystack and in Pantry, Fire Steps on left of Front Line; S.S.Line near Bley Farm. Pumping; Putting in Reynolds Orchard. PIONEERS Relaying Duckboards behind T.S.I & Avondale; Repair Wine Ave, Park Row, S.Line left of Burnt Farm. S.S. Line near Cowgate, Salop.	
		Night	R.E. Anchoring parties. M.G. Emplacements.	
	5.11.16	Day	Lieut Col. H.W. Gordon R.E. left the Company to take up appointment C.R.E. 58ᵗʰ Division R.E. S.Line. Parapet left of Estaminet; S.S. Line near Rt Batt⁰ H.Qrs. S.S.Line near Haystack and Pantry, Orchard, un left Bley Farm. Fire Steps on left of Front line, nr Salient. Pumping; Drain nr Reynolds Orchard. PIONEERS Relaying Wine Ave, Park Row, S.Line left of Burnt Farm, S.S.Line near Cowgate, Salop Ave.	
		Night	160 Infantry on Parapet of S.Line. R.E. M.G. Emplacements & Anchoring Parties.	
	6.11.16	Day	R.E. S.Line Parapet left of Estaminet; S.S.Line near Bley Farm and Haystack Ave & Pantry, Orchard, & near Rt Batt⁰ H.Qrs. Fire Steps on left of Front line; Pumping; Cleaning Conduit; Creating hut on horse line.	
		Night	PIONEERS Repairing & revetting Wine Ave, Park Row, S.Line left of Burnt Farm. S.S.Line near Cowgate, Salop Ave. 200 Infantry throwing up parapet on S.Line 160 Infantry throwing up parapet on S.S.Line. R.E. M.G. Emplacements & Wiring.	
	7.11.16		as for 6.11.11	Pioneers M.G. Implements
	8.11.16	Day	R.E. S.Line Front Line, Fire Steps in Salient SS.Line near Haystack Ave, Bley Farm, in Pantry, Orchard and nr Rt Batt⁰ H.Qrs. M.G. Emplacements & Pumping.	
		Night	PIONEERS S.S.Line 700.066. sh3 O.D & L.D. WSK. D.S.S. Forms C.2118. Relaying Duckboards, Sawing Tools & Stones. R.E. M.G. Emplacements. Wiring on S.Line; Pioneers M.G. Emplacements.	

Army Form C. 2118.

WAR DIARY
or
INTELLIGENCE SUMMARY.
(Erase heading not required.)

Instructions regarding War Diaries and Intelligence Summaries are contained in F. S. Regs., Part II. and the Staff Manual respectively. Title pages will be prepared in manuscript.

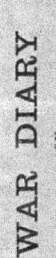
178TH FIELD COY.
No. ......
Date Feb 1916
ROYAL ENGINEERS

Place	Date	Hour	Summary of Events and Information	Remarks and references to Appendices
	9.ii.16	Day	RE S.S. line near Bier Farm, Avondale Rd, Haystack Ave, infantry Orchard, and run Rt Batt. Hd Qrs. Artillery on Left of Burnt Farm S. Line. Repairing front line, fighting Estaminet; Repairing London Bridge, Pump pit?	
			Pioneers Repairs to Park Row, S.S. line left of Burnt Farm. S. line; Salving tools, material etc. Rivetting Salop Ave. S.S. line near Cowgate.	
		Night	RE Front line right of Estaminet; Putting in dam in Courant; Putting outside parapet, Wiring on S. line. MG emplacement	
	10.ii.16	Day	RE S.line in front of Burnt Farm and on Left. S.line left of Rue du Bois; S.S. line near Bier Farm, at Avondale Rd. S. line M.G. Emplacement & Bomb pit. Draining London Bridge.	
			Pioneers S.S. line near Cowgate. S. line. Clearing bed of Courant. Salving tools & shires. Salop Ave.	
		Night	Infantry 2.00 on parapet of S. line. 160 on " " Rue du Bois.	
	11.ii.16	Day	RE M.G. Emplacements, wiring on S. & S.S. line.	
			R.E. M.G. Emplacements, Repairing S. & S.S. line & Rue du Bois. Putting in dugouts. Draining.	
			Pioneers On Coy relief. S. & S.S. line. Clearing bed of Courant. Repairing Salop.	
		Night	RE Wiring front on S. & S.S. line. M.G. Emplacements.	
	12.ii.16	Day	R.E. Repairs S. & S.S. line M.G. Emplacements. Repairs Rue du Bois. Draining. Preparing to move.	
			Pioneers. Clearing bed of Courant Repairs W.S. & S.S. line Salop & Cowgate.	
		Night	Infantry 160 on S. line & Rue du Bois.	
	13.ii.16	Day	Company preparing for move.	
		Night	Nil.	
	14.ii.16	Day	Company left Billets Rue Marle at 6.50 a.m. and marched to Vieux Berquin.	
		Night	Billets at Vieux Berquin.	
VIEUX BERQUIN IN RESERVE AREA	15.ii.16	Day	Company left Billets (V.B.) at 7.55 a.m. and marched to Reserve Billets arriving 11.15 a.m. Settling in.	
	16.ii.16		Drill and firing up Billets. Accompanied C.R.E. 34th D.V. round Camp in morning.	
	17.ii.16		2 Sections firing & batt hut repairing damage at No 5 Camp. 2 Sections Drill etc NCO's class.	Weather W. ball.
	18.ii.16			

B 2853 W. W8344/1454 700,000 5/15 D. D. & L.   A.D.S.S./Forms/C. 2118

Army Form C. 2118.

WAR DIARY
or
INTELLIGENCE SUMMARY.
(Erase heading not required.)

128TH FIELD COY.
No. ......
Date Feb 1916
ROYAL ENGINEERS

Instructions regarding War Diaries and Intelligence Summaries are contained in F. S. Regs., Part II. and the Staff Manual respectively. Title pages will be prepared in manuscript.

Place	Date	Hour	Summary of Events and Information	Remarks and references to Appendices
Reserve Area.	18.2.16.	A.M. P.M.	3 Sections Repairing damaged huts at Camp 6 & forming trestles, trestle huts & connecting preparing at Camp 2 & 6.	
" "	19.2.16.	A.M. P.M.	Physical drill, section drill, Rifle exercises. 3 Section deputed to build huts in infantry camps & trestles to baths. Lecture to NCOs by CSM.	
" "	20.2.16		Physical drill; Section till shipbuilders in repairing huts a trestles baths at infantry camps, altering work & repairs at R.E. Huts. Mounted section Routine work. Overhaul of Equipment; Wagons & Harness. NCOs Class	
" "	21.2.16		Physical drill. Work in infantry camps. Drill. Overhauling Equipment. Mounted Section routine work.	
" "	22.2.16		" " " " " " " " " " "	
" "	23.2.16	12.Noon	Moved to NEUF BERQUIN with 69th Infantry Brigade	
NEUF BERQUIN	24.2/16		Physical drill. Sect & Coy. drill. Rifle exercises. Lecture to NCOs by CSM. Mtd Sect Coy. drill & Routine.	
"	25.2/16		" " " " " " " " " "	
"	26.2/16		Returned to Reserve Area.	
Reserve Area	27.2/16		Off loaded wagons. General fleet.	
" "	28.2/16		Overhaul of outposts. Routine & trestle wagons. Saw overhaul of wagons. Drill. Inundatory initiation.	
" "	29.2/16		Left Reserve Area. Entrained at Caloone Ricouart, mounted section wagons marched. Bn marched to annexe Caloone Ricouart 11 a.m. Mounted section at 6 p.m.	

J. McOmmonne
Major R.E.
O.C. 128

3353   Wt. W3544/1454   700,000   5/15   D. D. & L.   A.D.S.S./Forms/C. 2118.

WAR DIARY
or
INTELLIGENCE SUMMARY.
(Erase heading not required.)

Army Form C. 2118.

128TH FIELD COY
No. ....
Date March 1916
ROYAL ENGINEERS

Place	Date	Hour	Summary of Events and Information	Remarks and references to Appendices
Colonne Ricouart	1/3/16		Standing fast. Physical drill chi pari: N.C.Os clean under C.S.M. Coys fatigue on billets.	
	2/3/16		" " " " " " "	
	3/3/16		Physical drill. Short route march. N.C.Os clean & routine work.	
	4/3/16		" " " " " Rifle revision, routine drill routine work. N.C.Os clean	
	5/3/16		" No 1 & 2 sections proceed to Gouy Servins work in R.E. dump. 3 & 4 sec to Route march	
	6/3/16		" Nos 3 & 4 Sec to cleaning up spots routes lowers. No 5 in road number limiers at Gouy Servins	
	7/3/16		Ready	
	8/3/16		7 oz 3 & 4 sects v HQ move to Villers-au-Bois	
	9/3/16		" " " " Gouy-Servins, Bruley Chilling tigetig lower at Seleck pointe attention	
	11/3/16		" " " " Villers au Bois, Shelters ready from	
	12/3/16		Company. Repairs walls to Division HQ's. Tunnels & approaches recommended by parties. Division HQ's & shelters	
Villers au Bois.	13/3/16		Road work	
	14/3/16		Road work & preparing frown Camps	
	15/3/16		Company move to Aix-Noulette	
	16/3/16		" " " to Rulty Aix-Noulette	
	17/3/16		Settling in at Aix-Noulette (Work in Tunnels on support & 2nd support line)	
	18/3/16 A.M.		M Stokepore & placemels ripara shiels.	
	" P.M.		Ri wall & support & 2nd support line	

Army Form C. 2118.

WAR DIARY
or
INTELLIGENCE SUMMARY.
(Erase heading not required.)

Instructions regarding War Diaries and Intelligence Summaries are contained in F. S. Regs., Part II. and the Staff Manual respectively. Title pages will be prepared in manuscript.

Stamp: 128TH FIELD COY. No...... Date Mar 1916 ROYAL ENGINEERS

Place	Date	Hour	Summary of Events and Information	Remarks and references to Appendices
Souchez Sector	19.3.16	A.M.	R.E. repairs to communication trenches.	
		P.M.	Infantry throwing up parapet on support line & Trench off H.Q.ᵗˢ Trench. Digging support trench.	
	20.3.16	A.M.	R.E. Repairing & revetting support line and second H.Q.ᵗˢ Trench.	
		P.M.	2/Lt. Capt A. Sutherland rejoined Coy. Transferred from 11th Cav.ʸ H.Q.ᵗˢ. Thde.	
		P.M.	R.E. Tchergun + Aerial Ropeman to place in revet., support line & N.E Q.ᵗˢ Trench R.E. repairs to revelled Infantry	
	21.3.16	A.M.	Throwing up parapet on support line & N.E Q.ᵗˢ Trench dug Trench.	
		P.M.	R.E. repairs to communication.	
			Infantry Digging & drawing support line. Throwing up parapet on support line & Thde. off H.Q.ᵗˢ Trench.	
	22.3.16	A.M.	R.E. Revetting & vavaelle support trench revet off H.Q.ᵗˢ Trench.	
		P.M.	Infantry Tut R.E. Repairs to communication.	
	23.3.16	P.M.	Infantry carrying on dig. & throwing up parapet Throwing up parapets & trenches in support line & H.Q.ᵗˢ Trench.	
	24.3.16	A.M.	R.E. Revet. & vavaelle Johans support line. Invett Thde off H.Q.ᵗˢ Trench.	
			R.E. Repairs to communication. Pioneers repairs to communication.	
		P.M.	Infantry 200 filling in revetments & digging in support + off Inf. Sap. H.Q.ᵗˢ Trench. Carrying thin.	
			Pioneers clearing drains & deepening communication trench. For support H.Q.ᵗˢ Trench & support line.	
	25.3.16	A.M.	R.E. Revet. & vavaelle support trench, making first Sap in N.E Q.ᵗˢ Trench.	
			R.E. & Pioneers Repairs to communication. drains	
		P.M.	Infantry & R.E. Carrying thin. Pioneers Fill. Weather very bad.	
	26.3.16	A.M.	R.E. & Pioneers Repairs to communication. ARRAS ROAD trench.	
		P.M.	R.E. Repairing and draining ARRAS ROAD trench.	
	27.3.16	A.M.	Infantry no carrying thin. Pioneers repairing Company Road. R.E. did not work owing to demolition to trench.	
		P.M.	R.E. Repairs to ARRAS ROAD. Pioneers Repairs to ARRAS ROAD.	
	28.3.16	A.M.	Infantry carrying thin. Throwing up count in revetments of H.Q.ᵗˢ Trench & support line.	
		P.M.	Pioneers (& eng.) Repairing & clearing Company Road & Sap & relieve N.E Q.ᵗˢ Trench & support line.	
	29.3.16	A.M.	R.E. Revet. making first H.Q.ᵗˢ Trench. Revetting vavaelle. Supporting Line. Wiring N.E. off very bad.	
		P.M.	R.E. Repairs to ARRAS ROAD. Pioneers repairs to ARRAS ROAD & Company Road.	
			Infantry Carrying thin fill. revets. & throwing up parapet off H.Q.ᵗˢ Trench & Support line.	
	30.3.16	A.M.	Pioneers Repair Company Road & Sap &. R.E. Revet. Support line. & Sap &.	
		P.M.	Pioneers Repairing Company Road Comps & Sap & (except Stocks fills in revets & deep. Group of H.Q.ᵗˢ Trench & support line	
			Infantry Carrying thin. Sitting & fill in revet. & deep. Group of H.Q.ᵗˢ Trench & support line.
			Pioneers 2353 Wt.P.25001/453 Dec 1000 D45 Rd. D&L.Ltd. D.S.S. Forms/C. 2118. Rev by Sap &.

WAR DIARY or INTELLIGENCE SUMMARY.

Army Form C. 2118.

128TH FIELD COY.
ROYAL ENGINEERS

Place	Date	Hour	Summary of Events and Information	Remarks and references to Appendices
Souchez	30.3.16	P.M.	R.E. Revett, making fire bays in H.Qrs Trench; Removal & draining Support Trench.	
	31.3.16	A.M.	Pioneers Repairing NBRRA's ROAD. Cleaning & deepening Company Road & Sap 6. Infantry Carrying Stores Repairing Support lines. Relieving wire Entanglements perepairing Support lines. Pioneers Repairing & Cleaning Company Road & Sap 6.	
		P.M.	R.E. Revetting drainings, revetting & making fire bays in H.Qrs Trench. Support lines. Repairing Traverses, wires in Hd Qrs Trench.	

JNArmstrong
Major RE
O.C. 128th Field Coy RE

WAR DIARY or INTELLIGENCE-SUMMARY

Army Form C. 2118.

128 FERE VOL 7

XXIII

Place	Date	Hour	Summary of Events and Information	Remarks and references to Appendices
AIX - NOULETTE	1.4.16	A.M.	R.E. Repairing Communication trenches. Pioneers Repairs ARRAS ROAD Tunnel; Company Road & Sap 6. Infantry Camp Duties.	
		P.M.	Engineering: Bagmaking. Digging & filling in trenches in Company Road & Sap 6. HQtrs=? on Support line. Pioneers Drains, defences, parapets, Company Road & Sap 6.	
	2.4.16	A.M.	R.E. Drawing & removing superstructure Sap 6 & H.Q.= Trench. R.E. Repairs ARRAS ROAD. Pioneers Repairs ARRAS ROAD. Repairs, clearing drains B. Company R.E. & Sap 6.	
		P.M.	Infantry:- Nil. Heavy shelling on ARRAS ROAD. Pioneers:- Clearing Company Road.	
	3.4.16	A.M.	R.E. Running & removing superstructure. Wiring & anchoring, making & improving trenches off H.Q.= Trench. R.E. Repairs ARRAS ROAD. Pioneers Repairs & clearing Sap 6.	
		P.M.	Infantry Parapeting ARRAS ROAD Tunnel. Carrying stores. Deepening & Supt. Coy Road Sap 6 & H.Q.= Trench. Pioneers Deeps & Draining Coy Road, clearing Sap 6.	
	4.4.16	A.M.	R.E. Tunnel Supt. Parapets superstructure H.Q.= Trench. Removal of unused supplies.	
		P.M.	Infantry Sap 6 & Company Road & ARRAS Road. Carrying stores. Rains. Parapets ARRAS ROAD, Dug outs, Supports line. Pioneers Sap 6 & Company Road. R.E. Rebuilding unused & tidying Supports line.	
	5.4.16	A.M.	R.E. Clean & deepen Sap 6 & Company Road: R.E. Fraistolpe & Plankwalks + tidying up H.Q. Trench.	
		P.M.	Pioneers Parapets ARRAS Road. Carrying stores. Supports line. Infantry Tiles revetment & Fraistolpe & HQ=Trench.	
	6.4.16	A.M.	Pioneers Sap 6 & Company Road. Removal of unused stores on Supports line. Wiring Richmond. HQ=Trench. Moreau Trench.	
		P.M.	R.E. Dugouts. HARAS Road (Western). Fraistolpe Plankwalks in Trenches off H.Q.=Trench. Pioneers ARRAS Road. Sap 6. Infantry Carrying stores, dugouts, supports line. Parapet ARRAS Road. Clean HQ=Trench & branch Moreau.	
	7.4.16	A.M.	Pioneers Cleaning Sap 6: R.E. Supports line Wiring, tiding HQ Trench Railway HQ=Trench & branch Moreau	
		P.M.	R.E. Fraistolpe supports line in H.Q.= Trench. Reinforcing parapets. Pioneers Sap 6, Company Road.	
			Infantry Carrying line. Parapet Arras Road. H.Q.=Trench & Pioneers Sap 6, Parapets Coy Road. R.E. Supports line. Wiring. Removing H.Q.=Trench branch Moreau Trench Moreau Trench.	

Army Form C. 2118.

WAR DIARY
or
INTELLIGENCE SUMMARY.
(Erase heading not required.)

Instructions regarding War Diaries and Intelligence Summaries are contained in F. S. Regs., Part II. and the Staff Manual respectively. Title pages will be prepared in manuscript.

Place	Date	Hour	Summary of Events and Information	Remarks and references to Appendices
Aix-Noulette	8.4.16	A.M.	Pioneers Repairs Arras Road. Clearing Sap 6 & R.E. Dump. Arras Road. Front Puitslips in H.Q^s Trench	
		P.M.	Infantry Buffs Front trench. Support line Reserve Trench. Carry John Pioneers Parapet on Company Road.	
	9.4.16	A.M.	R.E. Supporters; Wiring; Puitslips in Infantry. R.E. Dump Arras Road. Puitslips in front trench. Fn Puitslips of H.Q^s trench. From 7th W^s trench. Pioneers Reparations Arras Road. Dump about Sap 6.	
		P.M.	Infantry ditto. Supporters ditto. Infantry H.Q^s Trench. Pioneers Parapet Company Road. Sap 8. R.E. Supports ; Wiring ; H.Q^s Trench.	
	10.4.16	A.M.	Pioneers Arras Road repairs. R.E. Dump. Arras Road. Fire Trap H.Q^s Trench. Road Skin	
		P.M.	Infantry Skin. H^d Q^s trench. Puitslip in H.Q^s trench. Communication Trench from S line to F. line. Pioneers Company Road Sap 8; R.E. Ammt exper Ind trolley Infantry Wiring; Revett & dam	
	11.4.16	A.M.	Pioneers Arras Road. R.E. deep Arras Road. Puitslips & front line H.Q^s Trench. Road skin.	
		P.M.	Infantry Carrying Stores. Support line; Firstrap. H.E. Q^s trench. Buffs. Replacement of Stokes Gun Pioneers Sap 8 & Company Road. R.E. Supportline; Wiring; Puitslips.	
	12.4.16	A.M.	R.E. Arras Road & Mud Puddles; Coundery (Mined) dugout Arras Road.	
		P.M.	Weather too bad and no work.	
	13.4.16	A.M.	R.E. Arras Road. Puitslips in trenches & H.Q^s Trench. Pioneers Repy Phinkman in Sap 6; Coundery. Arras Road.	
		P.M.	Infantry Stores; Supportline; Revetting on front line. Pioneers Sap 8 & Company Road. R.E.	
	14.4.16	A.M.	R.E. Support line H.Q^s Trench. Replacement of Stokes Gun. Arras Road. Puitslips & front line. H^QQ^s Trench & Front line. Bomb shin Pioneers Arras Road Pioneers Sap 8. R.E. Arras Road. Puitslips & Stokes Gun.	
		P.M.	Infantry Carrying line. Pioneers Skin. Company Road Sap 8. Revett ; Puitslips intopparline ; Wiring ; Stokes gun Replacement ; H^d Q^s Trench.	
	15.4.16	A.M.	Coundery Arras Road. Pioneers Sap 8. R.E. Puitslips in Front line in H.Q^s Trench. Bomb shin deep in Arras Road.	
		P.M.	Infantry Skin. Communication trench between Support line. Pioneers Parapet Puitslips in H.Q^s Trench. Pioneers Sap 8 & Company Road. R.E. Support line in H.Q^s Trench. Good deal of M.G. & Shrapnel fire.	

Army Form C. 2118.

WAR DIARY
or
~~INTELLIGENCE SUMMARY~~
(Erase heading not required.)

Instructions regarding War Diaries and Intelligence Summaries are contained in F.S. Regs., Part II. and the Staff Manual respectively. Title pages will be prepared in manuscript.

Place	Date	Hour	Summary of Events and Information	Remarks and references to Appendices
AIX-NOULETTE	16.4.16.	A.M.	R.E. Fixed up infantry flooring, fixed up in HQ.s trench. Deepening Arras Road. Pioneers Church.	
		P.M.	Infantry Carrying. Infantry in Support line.	
	17.4.16.	A.M.	R.E. Deepening Helmer; Philippe in Rotten Row + HQ.s Trench; Bomb store. Cavalry Deepening Arras Road. Divisional Relief.	
		P.M.	Infantry Nil. Relief. R.E. Support line; Wiring.	
	18.4.16.	A.M.	R.E. Fixed up Rotten Row + HQ.s Trench. Bomb store. Cavalry Deepening Arras Road + Support Cable.	
		P.M.	R.E. Support line. Revetting, deepening & cleaning Hd Q.rs Trench Branch. Moreau Trench. Stokes Gun Emplacement.	
	19.4.16.	A.M.	Sapping Cy; Company Road + Sap 6. Arras Road. (N.D.L Spur). Infantry Carrying. Thin. Weather very bad. Little sleep in.	
			R.E. Arras Road. Fixed up Rifle Row + HQ.s Trench. Cavalry Dist. work over storms + weather.	
		P.M.	R.E. Support line + Hd Q.rs Trench. Sapping Cy. Company Road. Arras Road + Sap 6. Infantry Carrying	
			"Shi". Weather very bad and wind. Cleared wet sent	
	20.4.16.	A.M.	R.E. Repairs Arras Road. Fixed up in Rotten Row + HQ.s Trench	
		P.M.	R.E. Nil. Sapping Cy. Repairs to Company Road + Sap 6 + ANZAC Road. Infantry Carrying. Shoi	
			Company did not turn owing to the bad state of ground.	
	21.4.16	A.M.	Cavalry Deepening Arras Road. R.E. Fixed up Bank Row + HQ.s Trench.	
		P.M.	Infantry Carrying Nil. R.E. Support line. Weather improving but still wet. No 3 Section attacked to 47th Divn R.E.for work.	
	22.4.16	A.M.	Cavalry Nil Weather and Road. R.E. Repairs to Arras Road.	
		P.M.	Nil. Weather & ground work and traffic.	
	23.4.16	A.M.	Cavalry Dist. to Tank. R.E. Revetting Support line. Infantry up to Arras Road.	
		P.M.	Infantry Carrying thin. Full all day making up parapet in Support line. Support Cy. Clear. Company Road	
			Arras Road + Sap 6. R.E. Support line, Stokes Gun emplacement + latrines. Dugout in Bank ditch.	
	24.4.16	A.M.	Cavalry Deepening Arras Road. R.E. Repairs & clearing Arras Road. Sapping Cy. Arras Road. Company Road. Sap 6.	
		P.M.	Infantry Carrying thin. Full all day. Support line. Sap 6.	
			R.E. Support line; Stokes Gun emplacement. Dugouts.	
	25.4.16	A.M.	Cavalry Arras Road. clearing. Full all day Support line. R.E. Repairs to Arras Road. Sapping Company Arras Road. Sap 6. Company Road.	
		P.M.	Infantry Carrying thin. Full all day. Support line. Sapping Company Arras Road. Sap 6. Company Road.	
			R.E. Support line; Stokes Gun emplacement. Repairs Dugout.	

WAR DIARY
or
INTELLIGENCE SUMMARY.

Army Form C. 2118.

Place	Date	Hour	Summary of Events and Information	Remarks and references to Appendices
AIX-NOULETTE	26.4.16	A.M.	Cavalry draining Arras Road & laying cable. R.E. repairs to Arras Road & lining Carency drain, Deepening Supports & Communication trench.	
		P.M.	Filling sand bags. Sapping Company Arras Road S.2 End. Draining Carency Road Keep & R.E. Dug outs; Slothin from emplacement; revets communication trench. Infantry Revet & Build Shelters & Supports.	
	27.4.16	A.M.	Cavalry deepen Arras Road & laying cable. R.E. repairs Laying Pembroton Arras Road.	
		P.M.	" " Infantry Carency drain Shelters, parapet Supports & Sapping Sumps. Sapping Company Repairs Carency Road Arras Road S.S.2.1 & Sap 6. R.E. Communication Trench; Supports line; Shelters & emplacements. Wiring.	
	28.4.16	A.M.	Cavalry deepen Arras Road & Cable. R.E. Slope parapets Arras road. Infantry Carency drain; revets Supports. Sapping Company	
		P.M.	" " road & Arras Road S.2.1 & Sap 8. R.E. Supports line, Bayelle line, Wiring, dugouts. R.E. Arras Road.	
	29.4.16	A.M.	Cavalry Arras Road & cable. Infantry Carency drain; Sumps pts & parapets & Supports line. Sapping Company Arras Road S.2 End.	
		P.M.	R.E. Dugouts; Support line Bayelle line; Wiring; Cavalry distribution of Infantry cable. R.E. Arras Road & Arras Road & Cable.	
	30.4.16	A.M.	Cavalry Arras Road & cable. R.E. Arras Road & plumbwork; Infantry Carency drain; work on Supports line. Sapping Company Sap 8, Carency Road, S.2 End Arras Road R.E. Supports line; Communication Trench & Parallels, Wiring Bayelle line, dugouts.	
		P.M.		

J.N.F. Armstrong
Major R.E.
O.C. 1st R.E. Fd. Coy.

/26 Field Coy RE
Vol 8
128 F.C. R.E.
XXIII
May

WAR DIARY or INTELLIGENCE SUMMARY
Army Form C. 2118.

Place	Date	Hour	Summary of Events and Information	Remarks and references to Appendices
Aix Noulette	1.5.16	A.M.	Cavalry deepening Arras Road and laying Cable ; R.E. Plan boards in Arras Road. One Sect to work 47th Division	
		P.M.	Infantry Carrying stores. Filling sandbags; widening support line; building up parapet & parados.	
			Sapping Coy. Sap 8 Arras Road St. & Coy Road	
	2.5.16	A.M.	R.E. Support line. Wiring. Revetting. H.Qrs Trench boards. Moreau Trench	
			Cavalry. Arras Road & Cable laying. R.E. Plan boards in Arras Road. One Sect to work 47th Division	
		P.M.	Infantry. Carrying stores. Work on Support line. Cable Keeve. Arras Road Trench	
	3.5.16	A.M.	Sapping Coy. Arras Road & Company Road & R.E. Support line. Wiring	
			Cavalry. Arras Road & Cable laying. R.E. Plan boards in Arras Road. One Sect to work 47th Division	
		P.M.	Infantry Carrying stores. Digging drains. Filling emptying, building up parados & parapet, organising trenches	
			Sapping Coy. 2nd Lt. Smith. R.E. Revetting Support line. Moreau Trench boards. H.Qrs Trench. Moreau Trench	
	4.5.16	A.M.	Cavalry Arras Road Cable laying. R.E. Plan boards in Arras Road. Revetting H.Qrs Trench & work on Moreau	
		P.M.	Infantry Arras Road. Carrying Stores; Support line. Sapping Coy. Company Road; Sap & Arras Road & R.L.	
	5.5.16	A.M.	R.E. Support line. H.Qrs Trench. Wiring	
			Cavalry Arras Road laying Cable. R.E. Plan boards Arras Road. Revetting H.Qr Trench	
		P.M.	Infantry. Carrying Stores. Support line. Communication Trench & drain in St.	
	6.5.16	A.M.	Sapping Coy. Arras Rd, sect Road & Company Road. Sap & R.E. Support line. Communication Trench to Front line. Wiring	
		P.M.	Cavalry. Arras Road & laying Cable. R.E. Plan boards & drain Arras Road. Revetting H.Q. Trench & Moreau Trench	
			Infantry Carrying Stores. Support line. Communication Trench. Arras Road Parapet	
	7.5.16	A.M.	Sapping Coy. Company Road. Arras Road. Sap & R.E. Support line. & Communication Trench	
			Cavalry. Arras Road. Hangtrs. Cable. R.E. Plan boards. Arras Road. H.Qrs Trench to Moreau	
		P.M.	Infantry. T.L. Battalion. Retiring. R.E. Support line. v Communication Trench	
	8.5.16	A.M.	Cavalry Deepening Arras Road. Laying Cable; R.E. Support line ; R.E. Ruparap for mines & drainage	
		P.M.		
	9.5.16	A.M.P.M.	Moving to new area	
	10.5.16 to 18.5.16	A.M.P.M.	Company acting Salvage party. Work on 22 Cheminots Station & hutting of R&R. Company drill & work of Wagon etc. One Section at Petmin at work under Corps Cdant.	

126th Field Coy RE

Army Form C. 2118.

WAR DIARY
or
INTELLIGENCE SUMMARY
(Erase heading not required.)

Instructions regarding War Diaries and Intelligence Summaries are contained in F. S. Regs., Part II. and the Staff Manual respectively. Title pages will be prepared in manuscript.

Place	Date	Hour	Summary of Events and Information	Remarks and references to Appendices
AIX-Noulette Southern Sectn.	19.5.16	P.M.	Infantry-Carrying parties. H.d.Qrs Trench & Support line. Sap G. R.E. Superintending. H.d.Qrs Trench. Communication Trench.	
	20.5.16	A.M.	R.E. Arras Road Trench & Bomb Store.	
		P.M.	Infantry Carrying. Working on Hd.Qrs Trench. Supports & Further Communication Trench. R.E. Revetting, Hd.Qrs Trench. Superintending. Communication Trench. Wiring.	
	21.5.16	A.M.	R.E. Arras Road & Hd.Qrs Trench. German Artillery obtained direct hits on parapets & sandbags.	
		P.M.	In work as above over. Infantry battle artillery fire.	
	22.5.16	A.M.	Arras Road & Hd.Qrs Trench.	
		P.M.	Infantry Support. H.d.Qrs Trench.	
			R.E. Superintending. H.d.Qrs Trench. Clearing thy out. Princess Patricia Bay Bayonet line.	
	23.5.16	A.M.	Carrying & superintending at trench dump; R.E. Arras Road; H.d.Qrs Trench & Bomb Store.	
		P.M.	H.d.Qrs Trench. Bayonet Trench Dump. Infantry Rifle & Hand defence, a communication Trench. Clearing out D.Gs.	
			Bayonet line & ARRAS Rd. R.E. Superintending. Infantry Supports. H.d.Qrs Trench. Communication.	
			Trench Wiring. Buyouts. Wiring.	
	24.5.16	A.M.	R.E. (Sketch) Demolition. H.d.Qrs Trench. Supports. Communication Trench.	
		P.M.	Infantry Carrying. Hd.Qrs Trench. Bayonet. Supports. Communication Trench. R.E. Defence Scheme.	
			Bayonet line & Arras Road. R.E. Revet & reinstate stations. Support line. Hd.Qrs Trench. Wired up	
			Superline. Weather bad tonight thick mud.	
	25.5.16	A.M.	R.E. Revetting, Hd.Qrs Trench, Supports, Hd.Qrs Trench. Pioneers Handmade ARRAS ROAD v RATION Trench.	
		P.M.	Infantry. Went up into action. Pioneers Bayonet line between Ration Trench & Helping Sapper	
			Road. Communication from APPEARSON to BAYONET line.	
	26.5.16	A.M.	R.E. Wire line. Improve Supports. Hd.Qrs Trench	
		P.M.	R.E. Road clear H.d.Qrs Trench. Supports line	
			Infantry Bayonet line Helping Outbar. Carrying &the Communication Trench. Support & H.d.Qrs Trench.	
			Pioneers. Bayonet line & ARRAS Road. R.E. General supervision. Signal Station; Supports. etc.	
	27.5.16	A.M.	Infantry & H.d.Qrs Trench. Support. Clearing Dugouts.	
			R.E. Bat-Shir " " " "	
		P.M.		

126 5th A RE

Army Form C. 2118.

WAR DIARY

(Erase heading not required.)

Instructions regarding War Diaries and Intelligence Summaries are contained in F.S. Regs., Part II. and the Staff Manual respectively. Title pages will be prepared in manuscript.

Place	Date	Hour	Summary of Events and Information	Remarks and references to Appendices
Aix-Noulette Souchez Sector.	28/5/16	A.M.	Infantry: HQ 2nd Tunnel. Kellett Line. Northumberland Road. RE Bombers: HQ 2nd Tunnel. Charing X dug outs; HQ 2nd Tunnel. Kellett line.	
		P.M.	Infantry: Carrying station dug-out. Bairelle line. HQ Q5 Tunnel. Ammunition to Tower line from Support. Pioneers: Ditto work; RE: HQ Q5 Tunnel. Kellett Line; Tunnel repair station. Water supply; Wiring from Support line.	
	29/5/16	A.M.	Infantry: Charing dug outs; Dugouts. Helena Tunnel. Kellett in. Northumberland road. RE Bombers: Ditto job; HQ Q5 Tunnel + Support line. Northumberland road.	
		3 P.M.	Infantry: Carrying ditto; Kellett line; HQ Q5 Tunnel; RE. Dug outs. Northumberland road; Viewerpark station. Water supply. Mining Jaws & Supports. Pioneers: Bairelle line + Communication & Tramway Road.	
		3 P.M.	Arras Road.	
	30/5/16	A.M.	Infantry: Ditto. RE. Bombers. HQ Q5 Tunnel + Kellett line. Northumberland Road.	
		P.M.	Infantry: HQ. Pioneers: Arras Road. Bairelle + Communications to Arras Road. RE. Sig. Station. Wates supply; HQ Q5 Tunnel. HQ Q5 Tunnel. Northumberland	
	31/5/16	A.M.	Infantry: Carrying ditto. HQ Q5 Tunnel; Kellett line. Northumberland Road; RE Bombers. HQ Q5 Tunnel. Northumberland Road; Kelleta line. Dug outs. Charing X.	
		P.M.	Infantry: Carrying ditto. Kellett line. Dugouts. Communication Helena Tunnel. HQ Q5 Tunnel. Dug outs. Northumberland Road; Bairelle line + Communicating to Arras Road. Pioneers: Arras Road. RE. Water supply; HQ Q5 Tunnel. Wiring; Signal station. Kellett + Northumberland Road.	

J.N. Armstrong
Major RE
O.C. 126th

2353 Wt. W2544/1454 700,000 5/15 D.D.&L. A.D.S.S./Forms/C. 2118.

Army Form C. 2118.

128 F.E. RE

WAR DIARY
or
INTELLIGENCE SUMMARY.

(Erase heading not required.)

Vol 9 June

Instructions regarding War Diaries and Intelligence Summaries are contained in F. S. Regs., Part II. and the Staff Manual respectively. Title pages will be prepared in manuscript.

Place	Date	Hour	Summary of Events and Information	Remarks and references to Appendices
Aix-Noulette Sauchez South	1/6/16	A.M.	Infantry carrying parties, Kellerthein; HQ's Trench, Helmer, Bryant	
		P.M.	R.E. Bordeling, Watersupply Northumberland Road; Bryant Pioneer Infantry Carrying parties; Pipeline HdQrs Trench	
	2/6/16	A.M.	R.E. Thread supporting station HdQ'S Trench. Enemy M.G. & Shrapnel fire prevented work on support to 4th Communication [...]	
			Infantry Carrying parties; HdQ'S Bryant & Bryant; R.E. WaterSupply HQ= Trench	
		P.M.	Kellerthein Northumberland, Bryant Pioneer Infantry Carrying parties; Pipe line HdQ'S, Medical Aid, Northumberland Road, Helmer Trench, Right defenses, Borderline Pioneer Avenue Road; Supply line communications DPRRNE Road	
			R.E. Signal station completed; Watersupply; HdQ'S Trench N° Richard Road, HdQ'S Trench	
	3/6/16	A.M.	Infantry } same as for 2nd inst.	
		P.M.	Pioneer RE }	
	4/6/16	A.M.	Pioneer } same as for 2nd inst. Stolik ammunition to Relief	
		P.M.	RE }	
	5/6/16	A.M.	R.E. under Rdn Helfgs accoutrement same as for 2nd inst.	
		P.M.	are used down as for 2nd inst. Section 3 R.M.D RE gone for instruction	
	6/6/16.	A.M.	As for 5th inst	
		P.M.		
	7/6/16	A.M.	As for 5th inst. Infantry in addition dipping around Trench.	
		P.M.		
	8/6/16	A.M.	As for 6th inst. In party also dipper Trench around Western waybord	
		P.M.		
	9/6/16	A.M.	As for 5th inst.	
		P.M.	No Infantry. Rest in for 5th inst.	
	10/6/16.	A.M.	Infantry & RE same as for 5th inst. all took part in construction	
		P.M.	Pioneer detrenchment Reliews	
	11/6/16.	A.M.	As usual	
		P.M.	No work except on Pipe line who were covered to Ho HQ's Trench	

Army Form C. 2118.

WAR DIARY
or ~~INTELLIGENCE SUMMARY~~
(Erase heading not required.)

1/2d 2/3 London Field Coy RE

Place	Date	Hour	Summary of Events and Information	Remarks and references to Appendices
Aix-Noulette	12.6.16	A.M. P.M.	Preparing to move Handing Over Stores etc to 2/3 Lon.Terr. Engineers. Left Aix.	
La Thieuloye	13.6.16	A.M.	Arrived La Thieuloye. Resting.	
"	14/6/16	A.M. P.M.	Resting. Little Drill.	
"	15/6/16	A.M.	Left La Thieuloye. Marched to Verchin. Weather showery but clearing.	
Verchin	16/6/16	am	Left Verchin. marched to Matringhem.	
Matringhem	17-23		Trestle Bridging, general tramping. Divisional Field Day 19.6.16. Men stood march very well.	
"	24.6.16		Marched to Aire and entrained.	
En Route	25.6.16		Arrived Longeau. Marched Yzeux.	
Yzeux	26-30		At Yzeux. Standing fast. 29.6.16 Inspected.	

J.W. Hammond ?
Major R.E.
O.C. 1/2 Lon Field Coy RE

23 July
128. F.C.R.E.
Vol 10

Confidential.

War Diary
of
128th (Field) Company. Royal Engineers.
From 1st July 1916 to 31st July 1916.

(Volume XII).

Army Form C. 2118.

WAR DIARY
or
INTELLIGENCE SUMMARY.
(Erase heading not required.)

Place	Date July	Hour	Summary of Events and Information	Remarks and references to Appendices
LA HOUSSOYE	1st	—	The company marched from ALLONVILLE to LA HOUSSOYE and went into billets.	
MILLENCOURT	2nd		The company moved from LA HOUSSOYE to MILLENCOURT and went into billets.	
ALBERT	3rd		The company moved from MILLENCOURT to ALBERT - Taken on billets and once shared at BLUE VUE Farm F.5.c Central - and shoot by until 11.0 a.m. Return to billets in ALBERT.	
"	4th		No. 4 Section of Sappers moved with the Cemetery in FRICOURT WOOD X.25.d 3.4. & stood by returning to ALBERT at night.	
"	5th		In the afternoon the Company moved forward to the FRICOURT - CONTALMAISON Sunken road, to the trench from ROUND WOOD X.21.d.5.5 to SCOTTS Redoubt X.21.a.9.9. carrying Mining Stores. Major T.N.F. Armstrong R.E. went killed by shellfire.	
"	6th		The night was not long enough to bring up the stores & dumped along the trench. Lieut. Beran R.E. was wounded. The company returned to ALBERT in the early morning.	
"	7th	9.30 a.m.	The Company moved at the hour above about F.8.a.1.9. In the afternoon Nos 1, 2 & 3 Sections moved up to the trenches via Bn HQ about F.26.8.9. No 4 Section reported to 11th R. York at FRICOURT FARM. All 4 Sections did no work & returned to Bivouac in the Early morning of the 8th.	

WAR DIARY or INTELLIGENCE SUMMARY.

Army Form C. 2118.

(Erase heading not required.)

Place	Date	Hour	Summary of Events and Information	Remarks and references to Appendices
ALBERT Sheet 57D. SE & 62D. NE	July 8th		Captain P. ac Snellengu RE joined the Company in Command. No 4 Section of Sappers were in bivouac about F.2.c.0.0. Infantry to being sent forward to reconnaissance CONTALMAISON. In the absence of Captain - the Head Quarters & mounted Section were in billets in ALBERT.	
		1.0 p.m.	No 4 Sections Company 15 Sappers a man 4 addition to Pioke. Stocks- marts. Continues moved up to about F.2.6.7.9. & took by-Later in the situation did not permit of the Party occupation of the village. The new Distances Bivouac at F.2.00.00. for the night.	
	9th	1.45 p.m.	4 Section of Sappers returned to billets at ALBERT.	
	10th	10 a.m.	4 Section RE returned to bivouac at F.2.c.o.o. Received 23rd Div. CRE order No 58. Copy attached	Appendix I
			In accordance to this order No1 section marched at 2.0 p.m. for this position Assembly at X15e99. The remainder of the Company marched at 2.15 p.m. by the N.E. edge of BECOURT wood - + Aberdeen Communication Trench - thence deflecting to the Sunk Trench a harrage & working up to the Old German 2nd Line to its position Assembly at X21c5.9. Reported Progress up of 8th Bn about 4.15 p.m. & one No 1 Section had lost its way & had reported at Bde H.Q. No 1 Section Proceeded to Coy at X21c.5.8. At 7.30 p.m. orders were sent by Gol. 69th Bde for the Company to move up to CONTALMAISON. Which had been Captured. Routs taken from X21c59 to SUNKEN Road about X21d.5.5. Thence down trench along N. edge of BIRCH TREE WOOD &	

WAR DIARY or INTELLIGENCE SUMMARY.

Army Form C. 2118.

(Erase heading not required.)

Place	Date	Hour	Summary of Events and Information	Remarks and references to Appendices
ALBERT	11th		SHELTER WOOD – There were about 200 x officers & 0 SHELTER ALLEY which runs into CENTRAL MAISON. In this latter trench the 2 Companies 8th Yorkshires by two companies D. Yorkshire who were held up by a heavy curtain fire on the N. and of the trench. The Companies had to form some time in the trench which was very heavily shelled. Messages were continually being passed down the infantry that the R.E. were blocking their retirement – then it appears was ignored as they did not come. From an officer. Finally a message was delivered by a messenger importing them to the L.C. Infantry to the R.E. officer at the head of the trench ordering his retirement. His reason for the sapper's head across the sap through the barrage – Owing to delay in bringing along some wounded men, the whole of the Company did not reach Sunken Road until 12.30 a.m. on 11th as they had to wait to start up again and began work with the Companies returned to bivouac. at 1.30 p.m. Casualties 10th officer & 0 Other Ranks wounded. — Past	
		2.3 p.m.	On receipt of orders from C.R.E. the Company marched by FRICOURT, SUNKEN ROAD & SHELTER ALLEY to CENTRAL MAISON – arriving there 1.30 p.m. the Company was billeted in making a strong point at the "VIEUX MANOIR" X 17 c 2.8. Sketch attached. The Company left CENTRAL MAISON at 6.0 p.m. and returned to billets in ALBERT the same evening. No casualties. — Past	Appendix II
"	12th	2.0 p.m.	The Company marched to BAIZIEUX and went into billets in the Village. — Past	
BAIZIEUX	13th		Checking of equipment, fatigues and letters. Generally. — Past	

WAR DIARY
or
INTELLIGENCE=SUMMARY.

(Erase heading not required.)

Army Form C. 2118.

Place	Date July	Hour	Summary of Events and Information	Remarks and references to Appendices
BHZIEUX	14th	Morning	Inspection of Billets and company fatigues –	
		Afternoon	Drill – **Pat**	
	15th	Morning	Route march – followed by Coy. fatigues –	
		3.0pm	Hot baths for No 4 Section J.Saphers – **Pat**	
	16th	Morning	Church Parade	
		Afternoon	Company Sports **Pub**	
	17th	Morning	No 3 Section to ST GRATIEN for work under C.E. III Corps	
		6.30am		
		7.45am	Physical Drill & loading Pontoon Pyrite wagon	
		8.30am	Bridging wagon to ALBERT Redoubt for work under 227 & 228 A.T. Company	
		9.0am	Instruction & Drill with Smoke Helmets.	
		Noon	Inspection of No 1, 2, & 3 Section in Marching Order **Pat**	
	18th	2.0am	No 3 Section to ST GRATIEN for work under C.E. III Corps –	
		9.0am	Physical Drill – Platoon Drill – Section Drill – Quarter Duties – **Pat**	
			Remainder	
	19th	7.45 – 9.0am	Physical Drill –	
			Overhaul of Tool Carts. Cleaning, sharpening & testing of Tools & Instruments – Packing of Tool Carts in hand. – **Pub**	
	20th	Morning	Physical Drill – Section Drill and Interior Economy. Afternoon Lecture on Saluting to Officers NCO's.	

Army Form C. 2118.

WAR DIARY
or
INTELLIGENCE SUMMARY.
(Erase heading not required.)

Instructions regarding War Diaries and Intelligence Summaries are contained in F. S. Regs., Part II. and the Staff Manual respectively. Title pages will be prepared in manuscript.

Place	Date July	Hour	Summary of Events and Information	Remarks and references to Appendices
MARZIEUX	21st	morning	Physical Drill. Semaphore Signalling - Section + Company Drill - Carpenters making trestles for Kitchen - Pioneers repairing Company Carts + wagons - Rest	
	22nd	morning	Physical drill - Semaphore signalling and knotting + lashing. Inspection of Kit, arms + field dressings + iron rations - Rest	
	23rd	morning	Church Parade. The Company stood by to move at two hours notice until 10.30 a.m. Rest	
	24th	morning	Physical drill - Company stood by. No new orders. Sorting out men's kits. Stewart and Rees to duty. Rest	
	25th	morning	Semaphore - Physical Drill - Semaphore - training practice - Inspection of Smoke Helmets.	
		2.30 p.m.	No 2 Section marched to take over work + bivouac from McLartans La Company North of BECOURT CHATEAU - Remainder of Company packing ready to move -	
		4.30 p.m.	No 3 Section in truitiated [instructed] obtaining and enlarging sump pits - Relieving new pits for 1200 + along the HENENCOURT - BAZIEUX road.	
BECOURT WOOD	26th	8.30 a.m.	Company marched via HENENCOURT - MILLENCOURT - ALBERT & went into source in BECOURT WOOD N.25.d 5.4. Head Quarters + Transport P.S.60.2 - O.C. + 3 Officers went over work in progress on roads by My Lortland Field Coy R.E.	
		11 a.m.	Gas Alarm given - Coy roused + stood by with Gas helmets for 1 an hour - verified alarm from Fld Ambulance in BECOURT CHATEAU. At midnight as Fld line no sign of gas any. Turned in again - Rest	
		11.30 p.m.		

WAR DIARY
or
INTELLIGENCE SUMMARY.
(Erase heading not required.)

Army Form C. 2118.

Place	Date July	Hour	Summary of Events and Information	Remarks and references to Appendices
BECOURT WOOD	27th	7.30am	Company Paraded for work. No 2 Section Unloading G.S. & Bridging wagon, filling into Platform Material was & taking forward to CONTALMAISON — Nos 1 & 3 Sections repairs X-Roads CONTALMAISON to CEMETERY X17c 2.0 & Road for MT towards the QUADRANGLE — No 1 Section 1 man wounded. No 4 Section filling holes & repairing roads in CONTALMAISON — Pat	
	28th	7.30am	Company Paraded for work. 1 me carpenters & painters employed on making Contourmaps & notice boards. Remainder of the Company & 3 Bridging wagon on the CONTALMAISON — QUADRANGLE road — 2 Sergt Mr RANDERS rejoined for duty with the Coy— Pat	
	29th	7.30am	Company Paraded for work. Nos 1 & 4 Sections continued work on the Junction of the CONTALMAISON — QUADRANGLE Road between CONTALMAISON and the Cemetery. Nos 2 & 3 Sections started work on a Road from FRICOURT FARM to CONTALMAISON — from the FRICOURT Fm End. This road follows the route the JH Wood shown as existing on the map from FRICOURT FARM as far as S. end of SHELTER WOOD — Pat	
	30th	9.30am	Company Paraded for work. Nos 1 Section continued work on CONTALMAISON — CEMETERY road. Nos 2 & 3 Sections with 3 wagon for carting metal cont'd work on FRICOURT FARM Road. No 4 Section employed under C.R.E. & Divisional H.Q. & West of ALBERT. Pat	
	31st	7.30am	Company Paraded for work F. took a.a. on 30th inst. Pat	

Sd Lo Lorlangue
CapRE
OC. 128th (St) Coy RE

2353 Wt. W2544/1454 700,000 5/15 D. D. & L. A.D.S.S./Forms/C. 2118.

Appendix I.

COPY No. 2

<u>23rd Division - C.R.E. Order No. S.8.</u>

9.7.16.

(1) The 69th Infantry Brigade is to attack CONTALMAISON from the west tomorrow evening.

(2) One section of 128th Field Coy. R.E. will report to 9th YORKS Regt. at 3.30.p.m. on 10.7.16. at X.15.c.9.9. to assist in consolidation of a post at X.16.b.4.3. Route via. SNUSAGE Valley to X.20.b.4.3. and then up communication trench to above assembly point.

(3) The 101st Field Coy. less H.Q. and 128th Field Coy. less one section and H.Q. will assemble in trench at X.21.c.52 at 4.p.m. on 10.7.16. The 128th Field Coy. will leave one officer in billets to command the H.Q. of both Coys.

(4) On G.O.C. 69th Brigade informing Division when the Coys. are to move up, orders will be sent to them via 69th Bde. Advanced H.Qrs. at Scots Redoubt X.21.c.9.9. The 128th Field Coy. will consolidate the Manor House buildings at X.17.c.2.8. and the 101st Field Coy. will consolidate the vicinity of Cross Roads at X.16.d.8.4. The Coys. less one section 128th Field Coy. will report to G.O.C. 69th Infantry Bde. at Scots Redoubt for orders as to route to be followed into CONTALMAISON.

(5) The R.E. working parties in (2) and (3) will be withdrawn before dawn.

(6) Instructions re material will be issued later.

(7) One day's rations in addition to the Iron Ration will be carried.
Overcoats will not be carried.

(8) Reports to C.R.E. at Divisional H.Q. via H.Q. 69th Infantry Bde.

A.G. Bremner
Lieut: Colonel R.E.
C.R.E. 23rd Division.

IM

Issued at 7.00 a.m. 10/7/16 by messenger
No.1 copy to 101st Field Coy. R.E.
No.2 " " 128th " " "
No.3 " " H.Q. 69th Brigade.
No.4. " " H.Q. 23rd Division.

Appendix I

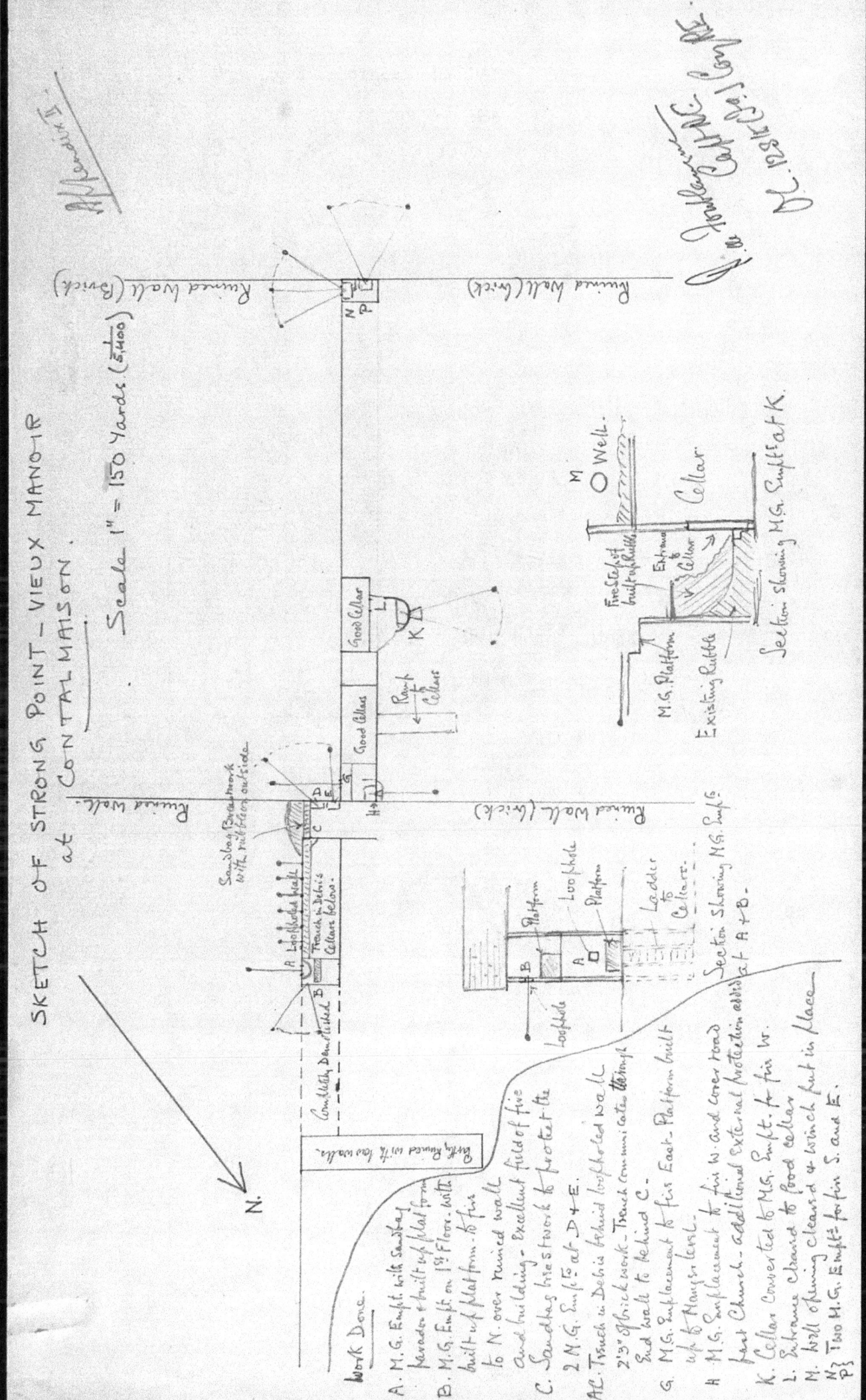

23rd Divisional Engineers

128th FIELD COMPANY R. E.

AUGUST 1 9 1 6

Vol 11

Confidential

War Diary
of
128th (Pioneer) Company, R.E.

from 1st August 1916 to 31st August 1916

(Volume XIII)

Army Form C. 2118.

WAR DIARY
or
INTELLIGENCE SUMMARY
(Erase heading not required.)

Instructions regarding War Diaries and Intelligence Summaries are contained in F. S. Regs., Part II. and the Staff Manual respectively. Title Pages will be prepared in manuscript.

Place	Date April	Hour	Summary of Events and Information	Remarks and references to Appendices
BECOURT WOOD	1st		No.1 Section continued work on the road from CONTALMAISON to CONTALMAISON CEMETERY. No. 2 & 3 Sections on the road from FRICOURT FARM to the S. end of SHELTER WOOD. No. 4 Section employed on erection of Brit. H.Q. West of ALBERT. (W27 C 2.8) Party of Carpenters making mining frames at DERANCOURT workshops – Pat	
"	2nd		Chinese & Bantam Platoons on the FRICOURT FARM road. No.1 Section was taken off the CONTALMAISON road & put on to FRICOURT FARM road with No. 2 & 3 Sections. No. 4 Section moved to DERANCOURT. Shot Guinswood R.E. Forward in the Slype on Dugout frames & mining casing – Pat	
"	3rd		Work on FRICOURT Farm road & in DERANCOURT workshops continued as a Pioneer day – Pat	
"	4th		Work on FRICOURT Farm road continued. 75 men from a Labour Battalion were sent to assist by D.C. 9812 A.T. Company R.E. Pat	
"	5th		Work on FRICOURT Farm road continued – details as started on 5th of hill 1/2 about 4.50 yards of road completed to this date. 50 men of Labour battalion assisted. No F.S.9/6 Sapper MILLER R.E. wounded by rifle grenade explosion by his pick. No. 4 section continued work in Derancourt Shops on Dugout frames Pat	

2449 Wt. W14957/M90 750,000 1/16 J.B.C. & A. Forms/C.2118/12.

WAR DIARY or INTELLIGENCE SUMMARY

Army Form C. 2118.

Instructions regarding War Diaries and Intelligence Summaries are contained in F.S. Regs., Part II. and the Staff Manual respectively. Title Pages will be prepared in manuscript.

(Erase heading not required.)

Place	Date August	Hour	Summary of Events and Information	Remarks and references to Appendices
BECOURT WOOD	6th		Work continued on FRICOURT FARM Road and Demancourt on Dugouts. Stood A.C. 94th T.M. Company and working parties both carried to this taking on. Pat	
	7th		Work continued as before. Returned to billets for dinner and in the afternoon looked out for men for mon - 10 officers and 12 men of the 94th (?) Coy. arrived in the morning as advanced party to take over work at billets. A handing over the work to 94th Coy. the road has been completed from FRICOURT FARM to SHELTER WOOD, and there about 2 way down the hill. with the exception of a small patch just in rear of that just at the top of the hill. Pat	
BRESLE	8th		Company paraded in marching order at 10.15 am. Handed (this no 4 sect. at DERNANCOURT) to BRESLE - and arrived with bivouac in that village (D15a 2.3) - No. 4 Sect. rejoined the company at BRESLE from DERNANCOURT. Billets and work at BECOURT WOOD were taken over by 94th (?) Coy. R.E. Pat	
	9th	9 hrs 4.0 hrs	Into to Economy. Orders from no 4 St. + I Corps Arras received. Great 8 this + 2 other ranks with bicycles entrained at MERCOURT as advance party for the company to the 17th Corps. Area. & accordance with below	

2449 Wt. W14957/M90 750,000 1/16 J.B.C. & A. Forms/C.2118/12.

Army Form C. 2118.

WAR DIARY
or
INTELLIGENCE SUMMARY
(Erase heading not required.)

Instructions regarding War Diaries and Intelligence Summaries are contained in F. S. Regs., Part II. and the Staff Manual respectively. Title Pages will be prepared in manuscript.

Place	Date	Hour	Summary of Events and Information	Remarks and references to Appendices
BRESLE	10th	5.15am	Whole Coys. & other ranks with transport left on advance of party for 11th Coy. R.E. Tok Asa.	
		9.30pm	Wind Christie with all transport and horses proceeded by march route to AILLONVILLE en route for VAUCHELLES LES QUESNOY.	
"	11th	12.40am	H.Q. & 9 dismounted sections marched to MERICOURT Station and detrained.	
		10am	Detrained at PONT RENY and marched to VAUCHELLES LES QUESNOY - billeted in the village.	
"		8pm	Transport arrived by march route from AILLONVILLE. No concern taken.	
"	12th		Nothing to record. Fatigues & bathing parades.	
"	13th		No work. Church Parade & Inspection. Bathing Parade.	
		6.0pm	Transport left by march route for LONG PRÉ les CORPS SAINTS Station. Parade in morning. Packing up in afternoon.	
		8.0pm	Sappers " " " " Station. 2d on arrival.	
	14th	12.40am	Company left by train for BAILLEUL.	
		11am	Company arrived at BAILLEUL. Extra dinners issued. Station & then moved by march route to MONT des CATS and went into billets.	
MONT des CATS	15th	10am	Sue Madrassa party with O.C. Company arrived at billets. 233rd (O) Coy. R.E. at ABEELE/HOPPE. Advanced party took over billets. O.C. took over work in hand by 233rd Coy. in return.	

2449 Wt. W14957/M90 750,000 1/16 J.B.C. & A. Forms/C.2118/12.

Army Form C. 2118.

WAR DIARY
or
INTELLIGENCE SUMMARY
(Erase heading not required.)

Instructions regarding War Diaries and Intelligence Summaries are contained in F. S. Regs., Part II. and the Staff Manual respectively. Title Pages will be prepared in manuscript.

Place	Date August	Hour	Summary of Events and Information	Remarks and references to Appendices
MONT des CATS	15th		Of line from CARTER'S FARM (Sheet 36 NW) C1od 1.2½ to SAPE "(Exclusive)" this sheet 28 Sh.r. 6.3.3 U 28 c 3.3 — Plan of Trenches attached —	Appendix I
	16th	10 am	Company arrived by March route from MONT des CATS at PONT de NIEPPE and went into billets vacated by 233rd Coy. RE at the latter place — O.C. Coy and section Officers went round work accompanied by line — Started work by day on the following; see map of Trenches. 1. Resuming Continuation of footwork lacking up HIGH COMMAND Posts behind GAPC 2. Completion of Supervision Trench behind 97 Trench. This Trench is being made with 5' U Frames [sketch: 6' / 5'], instead of infantry and Pioneers instead of being lined with Small semicircular steel dug outs at 12" intervals — A communication trench with this similar dug outs — four every 20 yds of this kind of the Supervision Trench — Men to have to stop to relieve fire — Support & Communication Trenches & 8th approach [?] routes, it is not proposed at the moment that left work already started on the Supervision trench and to cache half on the more essential trenches. 3. Support line behind 98 Trench — This is being restored and strengthened where necessary by U frames with Lois style. Sandby, revetment being used about this. O.C. U frames have to be the necessary additional height —	

WAR DIARY or INTELLIGENCE SUMMARY

Army Form C. 2118.

Instructions regarding War Diaries and Intelligence Summaries are contained in F. S. Regs., Part II. and the Staff Manual respectively. Title Pages will be prepared in manuscript.

(Erase heading not required.)

Place	Date August	Hour	Summary of Events and Information	Remarks and references to Appendices
PONT A MARCQ	27th		4. Cheshire Avenue – This had been constructed on A V frames (7') and consequently too narrow to work round finished. Coil this Company started to work of completion. Walls are rabbity V frames together there already, but in as it is found that the frames are not strong enough to stand the pressure if work if put in at present interval than 3 feet. 5. SCREEN AVENUE – Much work had been done in this avenue which is of tasks to form a by-pass where LE TOUQUET Station is being shelled. Dugouts in the cars were also at too great an interval. This company started work on continuing the framing (7' V frames) and inserting of this avenue - to strengthen the Revetting put in work had started on anchoring back the tops of the frames together. 6. Work continued on a dug Concrete M.G. dug-out - entrance of dug-outs. 7. Work continued on a cement 15" mould dug-out to excavations + a Shell Shelter. The cement floor had been completed by the previous division. Parties of this Company continued. Sites for a proposed work in the centre of	Appendix II Appendix III
PONT A MARCQ	28th			

2449 Wt. W14957/M90 750,000 1/16 J.B.C. & A. Forms/C.2118/12.

WAR DIARY or INTELLIGENCE SUMMARY

Army Form C. 2118.

Place	Date	Hour	Summary of Events and Information	Remarks and references to Appendices
ANTRA NIEPPE	18th/19th 19th		Gap C was reconnoitred. Work continued. The front line & the proposed locality in GAP C was allotted amongst & working parties were employed as follows — 108 Inf. by day — 150 by night working at SCREEN AVENUE.	
	20th		Work on all fronts continued — Inf. 195 by day on all 19th — 400 parties of SCREEN AVENUE by night M- 30 parties of HIGH COMMAND breastwork — OC Coy kept round the breastwork in same front with the GOC 68th Bde —	
	21st		Work continued — Inf. 200 by day — 200 by night on SCREEN AVENUE — 80 by night on HIGH COMMAND and GAP C, 60 by night parties of CHESHIRE AVENUE. O.C. Coy Right command Left Battalion went with the C.O. & Coy commanders & arranged for work to be started on the Strengthening of front line trenches with V frames & arranged for raising the floor boards — Also M.D. & Sapper allotted to each of the 3 Coys in the front line for supervision.	
	22nd		Work continued on all 1065 181 Infantry employed by day 360 by night —	
	23rd		Work continued on all Nos but 9382 which having been framed in pair as Long Avenue was stopped in order to concentrate on Gap C. O.C. Coy reconnoitred the Testor to the OBE. Inf. employed by day 245 — By night 250 —	

Army Form C. 2118.

WAR DIARY or INTELLIGENCE SUMMARY

(Erase heading not required.)

Instructions regarding War Diaries and Intelligence Summaries are contained in F.S. Regs., Part II. and the Staff Manual respectively. Title Pages will be prepared in manuscript.

Place	Date	Hour	Summary of Events and Information	Remarks and references to Appendices
PONT du HEM	24th		Work as usual continued. Night work on laying of SCREEN AVENUE also continued. Wiring Flank of main - Infantry Employed. By day 265 - By night 140 - Sap	
	25th		1 Casualty noted. Fatigues in the morning - Bathe in the afternoon. This day one Whizbee was taking place in the trenches, & the howitzer is being fired along the St Corps to St Ravoy Baro Relief day - i.e. once in 8 days. Sap	
	26th		Work continued as usual 285 inf. employed by day. 160 by night. Sap	
	27th		Work continued - Reclamation of WATLING AVENUE STREET started. 290 Inf Employed by day. No night work owing to installation by Special Bde R.E. taking place. Sap	
	28th		Work continued. Earthing up of D.M.G. Emplacements in front line Continued. Starter and Reclamation of BARNEHAM Avenue to this stage at intervals to Corin Gap B & Sub A Started. 300 Inf. Employed by day. No night work for reasons given above. 97 September trench Completed. Sap	
	29th		Work Continued. Cleaning of Entrenching tools started. No night work owing to weather. (Heavy Rain.) 315 Infantry Employed clearing day. Sap	
	30th 31st		Work continued - Weather very wet - no night work - 260 Infantry employed by day. Sap Work continued on all M.Gs - Earthing up of CHESHIRE Avenue stopping. T leads started by night. Sap Captain G.H. WE OC 178th Tunnelling Coy R.E.

Appendix II

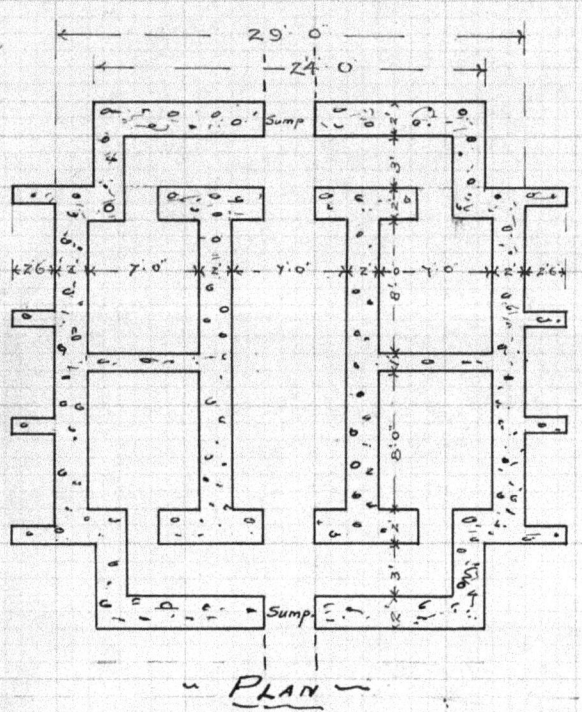

Note:- All concrete reinforced with ¾" & ½" rods.

~ Scale ⅛ inch = 1 foot. ~

vol 12

2?

Confidential

War Diary
of
120th (Field) Company RE

from 1st September 1916 to 30th September 1916

(Volume XIV)

Army Form C. 2118.

WAR DIARY
or
INTELLIGENCE SUMMARY

(Erase heading not required.)

Instructions regarding War Diaries and Intelligence Summaries are contained in F. S. Regs., Part II. and the Staff Manual respectively. Title Pages will be prepared in manuscript.

Place	Date	Hour	Summary of Events and Information	Remarks and references to Appendices
Pont de NEPPE	Feb 4th 1st		Front Garrison as usual. Rob	
"	2nd		Brigade Relief. The company rested - Clothes had in morning - Baths in afternoon. Orders received to move the next day. Rob	
HAZEBROCK	3rd		Company marched at noon and billeted at X 2 D 7.9 (Sheet 27) - arrived in the afternoon -	
			O.C. Company stayed behind & had on the road in horses to O.C. guard party Coy. by which Coy. this am was relieved. Showing App. of hazebrouck spent attached - Rob	Appdx. I
"	4th		Interior Economy. O.C. rejoined in afternoon - having been round the sector & the lines handed over with the O.C. of officers of the Relieving Company - Rob	
BLEUE MAISON	5th		Entrained at BAILLEUL - detrained at ST OMER - marched to BLEUE MAISON & billeted. Rob	
	6th		Fatigues & interior Economy - Rob	
	7th		Drill - Semaphore & fatigue. Rob	
	8th		Interior Economy - Nothing worthy recording - Chains harrow etc - Rob	
	9th		Alter to Economy J.D.	
	10th		Packing Wagons - Entrained at ARQUES (near ST OMER) at 11.35 p.m. Rob	

WAR DIARY or INTELLIGENCE SUMMARY

Army Form C. 2118.

Place	Date	Hour	Summary of Events and Information	Remarks and references to Appendices
ALLONVILLE	11th	9.15	Detrained at SALEUX (S. of AMIENS) & marched to ALLONVILLE & billeted. Rest	
BRESLE	12th		Marched from ALLONVILLE to BRESLE & billeted. Rest	
BECOURT	13th		H.Q. & 2 Sections marched to BECOURT wood & bivouacked at X.27 & 28 Clear (Ruins) 57 D SE.) For work under CRE 15th Div. One Company of 9th S. Staffd. Regt. (Pioneers) attached to assist in the afternoon. M. Coy with the 2 Section attached to (?) OC of the River Coy, reconnoitred to work, which was the continuation of a Becourville Tramway from about X.11.6.1.2 in the direction of MARTIN PUICH.	
"	14th	Mid.day	Left field 28th last crossroads at X.6 c.7.2. Nos 3 & 4 Sections marched to LA BOISELLE & reported to 2nd Northumbrian Fd/Coy. — Sett Dn ? "hello Himmock" X.27 c.55 Rest advanced to 2 shafts. Beef R.E. & 2 platoons Pioneers from 5.0 am to 11.0 am & 2 Pioneers Rest Party from 11.0 am to 5.0 pm. This was dug in order of today to town of work on Becourville Track can only be laid forward with consecutive working like this. with 1 Platoon Pioneers on carrying. 1 on making formation - & R.E. on track. Progress found that at out 350 J. of 16th Becauville consoldated laid in 12 hours. Nos 3 & 4 Sections & 1 company pioneers repaired tramway (old German) from vicinity of BOTTOM WOOD. to N. edge of MAMETZ WOOD - made it passable for handtrucks today. - Rest	

Army Form C. 2118.

WAR DIARY
or
INTELLIGENCE SUMMARY
(Erase heading not required.)

Instructions regarding War Diaries and Intelligence Summaries are contained in F. S. Regs., Part II. and the Staff Manual respectively. Title Pages will be prepared in manuscript.

Place	Date	Hour	Summary of Events and Information	Remarks and references to Appendices
BECOURT	15th		Nos 1 & 2 Sections returning, informed that no work on account of forward operation. OC Coy saw Officer i/c 7th I. Sheforts (Pioneers) taped out a road forward for tramway which was closed to receive for night work. Night work in not advised. No 3 & 4 Sections carried on their work now all in extension position. Light tramway track now taken up from tramway head BELLEVUE Farm (E.5.c. Sheet 62ⁿᵈN.E.) and laid between front X.18.a.8.3 (N.W. of MAMETZ Wood) and S.14.b.25. (Sheet 57D S.W.)	Rod
	16th		Nos 2 Section & 1 Company of Marines continued work on "Formation" - laying track & tying it up - for tramway towards HARTZNWICH - Work hindered by shelling. 6 Pioneers wounded - No 1 Section continued laying track in afternoon at 6 Sheet S. Formation - very little hostile enemy R shelling on ridge about X.6.C.9.3. No 3 & 4 Sections continued work on their tramway - who went in exceptional shell fire -	Rod
	17th		No 2 Section & 1 Platoon Pioneers Continued work in morning - entered that shell-fire. No 1 Section or 3 Platoon Pioneers worked out at night - very satisfactory progress made. Nos 3 & 4 Sections continued work on their tramway -	Rod

2449 Wt. W14957/Mgo 750,000 1/16 J.B.C. & A. Forms/C.2118/12.

Army Form C. 2118.

WAR DIARY
or
INTELLIGENCE SUMMARY

(Erase heading not required.)

Instructions regarding War Diaries and Intelligence Summaries are contained in F. S. Regs., Part II. and the Staff Manual respectively. Title Pages will be prepared in manuscript.

Place	Date	Hour	Summary of Events and Information	Remarks and references to Appendices
BECOURT WOOD	18th		Work on tramway continued to Kephadiorate. No 3 & 4 Sections reported Company to bivouac.	
"	19th		Work on tramway continued until held up by lack of tramway track. The company moved to BILLETS in BECOURT WOOD – Ration drawn from 73rd Division R.E. × 25d 2.7.	
"	20th		Nos 1 & 2 Sections continued work on tramway – work still stopped by lack of track. No 3 Section started work on clearing GORDON ALLEY – Hindered by shellfire. No 4 Section workmen in command of billets.	
"	21st		Nos 1 & 2 Sections continued work on tramway. No track yet available for use. No 3 Section continued clearing GORDON ALLEY. No 4 Section started work on tabletting the tramline in SHELTER VALLEY and on making a siding and quarry in SHELTER VALLEY from which to draw chalk ballast.	
"	22nd		Work continued on tramway – Carrying track forward & ballasting. Work started on fixing 400 gallon tanks to flat trolleys – Bivouac in BECOURT WOOD was shelled between 7.30 & 7.30pm Casualties 1 Sergeant Killed ∧ Corporal died of wounds Smith wounded Bivouac again shelled about 9.30pm. No Casualties. Clearing of GORDON ALLEY after argument finished. Reb	
"	23rd		Work continued on tramway. No 3 Section Instants tramway & started 2× cavalry & new chalk × 16d 9.4. Reb Quarry broke up tools about this × 16d 9.4. Reb	

WAR DIARY
or
INTELLIGENCE SUMMARY

(Erase heading not required.)

Army Form C. 2118.

Place	Date	Hour	Summary of Events and Information	Remarks and references to Appendices
BECourt WOOD	24th		Work continued. Railhead a new post TANGLE Trench. Laid points for new Siding Quarry about X 10.d.9.9. Put in level crossing on FRICOURT CONTALMAISON road - & formed portion of tramline to present rop as road. Pat	
	25th		L.M.C work class - The Romans was not available in the morning. - & work was stopped in time to allow all parties to clear CONTALMAISON by noon, as operations were being undertaken on the Division front.	
	26th		Nos 1, 2, & 3 Sections left off work in time to clear CONTALMAISON by noon - wires of offensive operations or the immediate right - No. 4 section in SHELTER Valley continued at work - A Decauville Patrol Tractor arrived and an N.C.O. & man in charge - & was housed in the quarry in SHELTER VALLEY. Pat	
	27th		No 4 Section started work down - Remainder at 9.0 a.m. Work proceeded satisfactorily and the Patrol Tractor worked well - 1 Man wounded by Artillery fire. Pat	
	28th		Continued work on Tramway track and ballasting. Completed construction of 5 trestles - tent holdings - Started enclosed siding for tipping trucks. Pat	
	29th		Track completed to limit M 32 a 4.7. Tracing attacked. Continued ballasting & making loops & ciaings. Romans continue for special work. Pat	
	30th		2 sections stood by under orders near ALBERT & SHELTER VALLEY. 4th sections Hampshire & Armstrong huts from D.H.Q. Hd Qr ALBERT. 2 section continued for planks. 1 section night work. Were transferred to No 10 Coy R.E. the next about X 66 85. Pat	A/Lieutenant R Gilbey RE O.C. No 12th Coy R.E

Handing Over Report **Appendix I.**
85th Coy RE to 94th Coy RE

3rd Sept. 1915.

The Sector of the line in which this Company is working extends from the River LYS - on the right flank to the left of Gap 'E' on the left flank, the left of the sector line being the intersection of the RIVER WARNAVE with CHESHIRE Avenue.

The following work is in progress:—

1. **Defended Locality in Gap 'C'.** The front line is already in hand - & on its completion it is proposed to add two flanks - Each of about 2 firebays - and a Gorge containing dug outs (baby Elephants). A communication trench has been roughly dug - but not revetted - connecting this work to the High Command Breastwork in rear. It is proposed to use 5' U frames for this work.

2. **High Command Breastwork.** A breastwork forming the 3 High Commands in rear of Gap 'C' was started by our predecessors. Such part as is nearly complete stands up as a monument of conspicuous height. It is proposed to continue this breastwork - but with a lower command. It has been excavated nearly through - and the left hand end has been framed & partially earthed up. A communication trench runs through this breastwork to the Gap 'C' work - It is proposed to make this trench in the form of two long "straights" prepared for fire in either direction thus:—

```
        Gap 'C' Work      Gap C
      ───┬─────────      ─────
         │
         │
         │
         │
      ───┴─────
      High Command B'work.
```

3. **Trench 93S.** This has been framed and revetted by some previous division – but the work is hurried & rough, and the corners of the trench in particular need attention before winter.

4. **SCREEN AVENUE.** This is nearly complete. Corrugated iron (single sheet) is being substituted for expanded metal at the bottom of the trench in some of the latest work done. The drainage of the trench just N. of the MOTOR CAR Corner – WIDOW'S HOUSE road needs attention. The Divisional drainage officer has been taking the levels here & finds that by deepening the road-ditch on the South of the road for 1' – and by putting a drain through under the road – he can run the water from this portion of SCREEN AVENUE down to the main drain to the L×S.

A – Point in Screen Avenue where drainage is difficult
B C – To be lowered 1 foot and a box drain put in from A to B. 1' below present level of drain at B.

It will be necessary to consider all the points where drains cross SCREEN Avenue carefully – since the trench has been dug lower than the drains.

5. BARKENHAM AVENUE. Work has been started on reconstructing BARKENHAM AVENUE from its junction with 91S to STATION REDOUBT. It is being firestepped wherever the bends in the trench enable fire to be brought on to GAP 'B' & GAP 'A'. The trench is only being revetted where the present revetment is obviously unlikely to stand up.

6. Trench 91S requires attention in many places. No work has been done on it by this division – but a start has been made in one or two places by the previous division.

7. 97 S, 98 S, 99 S. work is in hand reconstructing the worst bays of this trench. and in traversing 98 S + 99 S where not already traversed. Standard Low U frames - with fire steps are being used.

8. ~~CHES~~ WATLING STREET (98 C.T.A) has just been framed and revetted sufficiently to prevent the bottom falling in. this is practically complete - 2 men can finish the work in one day. Protection from view is obtained from front parapet. If protection from fire is required the sides will have to be built up.

9. CHESHIRE Avenue from SUFFOLK Avenue to the river WARNAVE. This has just been reconstructed & patched up - parts of it had previously been framed & revetted - but the frames put in at too great interval - & they have consequently sprung. All Standard U frames are calculated for 3' intervals only.

3 T heads have just been started - to bring fire on Gap 'E'. One night's work only has been done. A mistake has been made on the right hand T head - digging was commenced on the wrong site - & then moved - the right hand effort should therefore be filled in - thus:-

(diagram: T-head sketch with note "to be filled in" — Cheshire Trench)

The T heads are sited just behind the crest. So that with an 18" parapet they will just be able to fire over the crest when the grass dies down. They are intended to be dug 3'. and chained into the Trench.

(diagram: cross-section showing Ground Line, Communication Trench, CHESHIRE AV., and T head)

CHESHIRE Avenue still needs finishing up.

10. M.G. Dugout. Long Avenue. All concrete work finished. Design attached.

11. Regimental Aid Post NICHOLSONS Avenue. Rough Design attached. Concreting not yet half finished. It is proposed to drain this by the Entrance & Exit trenches – which will have to be drained into NICHOLSONS Avenue – & that graded down to the JTrss Drain. There is a fall from the bottom of exit trench to bottom of drain of 22". I had proposed to dig out NICHOLSON Avenue & put in frames.

12. <u>Subsidiary Line</u>. I have recently started clearing & revetting this with some men of the Entrenching Bttn. Work has been started between RABEQUE Stream & MOTOR CAR CORNER road – & between LONG AVENUE & LYS Farm. This latter is of some importance if LYS Farm is to be held in the WINTER as a strong point on the right flank, as it is the only communication to it. I have done no work on LYS FARM – but the reconstruction of the trench to the N.W. of it has been taken in hand by someone fairly recently & is incomplete.

13. Repairs to steam pipes &c at PONT de NIEPPE Divisional baths.

———

The division has been in such a short time that little work has been initiated. I have been agitating for the reclamation of FORT DUDLEY to cover Gap E – it is at present derelict but its reclamation is not a big business. It is also proposed to put a low command fire trench behind the hedge running from C4a 2½.5 to C4a 4.3. to cover the back of GAP D.

I asked for two reports on roads. one the MOTOR CAR
CORNER to front line road - & the other the
GASOMETER CORNER to FRONT Line road.
The CRE called for these reports with a view
to making preparations for the repair of
the roads in the event of an advance.
I consider the estimates for the second road to
be very excessive. They might I think be
reduced by ½ or ⅓.

Suggestion for lighting each Bn HQ with
neighbouring dugouts & Regs. Aid Posts with
Electric Light has been passed to CRE.

14. In addition to work carried out by RE. the Infantry
has been working on their front line - with
RE Supervision - particularly in 97. 98 and
102.

15. Minor repairs due to rain are required in
several places - notably FORT PAUL & SUFFOLK
Avenue.

16. Seven Fosse Redoubt needs attention when time
is available.

17. <u>Water Supply</u> Water from a well in Le TOUQUET
STA. is pumped into tanks & run by gravity
through 2" mains. (a) to a tank at the head
of LONG AVENUE. (b) to the
neighbourhood of BARKENHAM Fm. This latter
main is always giving trouble - I have been having
the leaks systematically repaired. & a tank
has been indented for by RE Yard - Armentières.
but it has not come. the main now ends in a
tap. Should this supply yield there is a
well in WIDOW'S HOUSE and another dug
by RE in 91 CTC at C.10.a.8.7. the quality of
the water from these two latter wells is in dispute among
the medical people.

18. All work now in hand is done by day except
   (1) Earthing up HIGH COMMAND & revetting it.
   (2) Earthing up GAP 'C' work
   (3)   "   up CHESHIRE Av. & digging T. heads
   (4) Mending BARKENHAM Pipe Line –

19. A list of Scissors required & existing – both having is attached. It has just been received & no work has been done on it.

20. Excavation for H.G. Concrete dugouts similar to the one being made in LONG AVENUE have been made at the S. E. of WATERMEAR Row and about C.37.5.2½. No concreting has yet been started.

Stores
   There are two advanced dumps –
   Right Subsection —— WIDOWS HOUSE
   Left   "   GUNNER'S FARM
   Stores are sent up to them by night by wagon – I supply the Brigade from these dumps –
   The Tramway in Corp. Ms & has just been connected through with GREAT NORTHERN & CALEDONIAN – which serve these advanced dumps – It remains to arrange with the Traffic manager to run you a daily train or trains.
      I attach a few notes on stores & administration –

Maps
   List of maps handed over is also attached –

3-9-16.

                                    Jas Fonblanque
                                       Capt RE
                                    O.C. 172th (S) Coy RE

List of Maps handed over to
94th (Fd) Coy R.E. by O.C. 128th (Fd) Coy R.E.
3.9.16.

Scale	Description	No.
1/5000	Trench map on paper	1
Do	Do Blue prints	2
Do	Do Cloth tracing	
	Trenches not shown	1
1/500	Detail map of gap C.	4
1/1000	Do Do Do	1
1/5000	Trench map cloth tracing	
Do	Drainage map on paper	1
1/5000	Heliograph map of trenches	2
1/5000	Blue print Do Do	2
Large scale paper tracing of front line from Essex H° to Railway		1
1/5000	Cloth tracing trench map (new)	1
	Blue prints of Ry- O.P. plan + Artillery O.P.	2
1/10,000	Trench map 36 N.W. 2	1
Do	Do 28. S.W 2+4	2
Do	Do Do 4	2
Do	Do 36 N.W. 2 + N.E. 1	2
1/40,000	France 36	1
Do	Do 36ᴬ	1
1/20,000	Trench Map 36 NW	5
1/20,000	Do 28 SW.	5
1/10,000	Do 28 S.W. 4	1
	" " Ed 3D	2
1/40,000	Secret tracing on paper	1

4 Rough Trench Maps.

G.A.P. Brown.
Major RE
O.C. 94th Fd Coy RE

3-9-16.

SCALE OF Yds. 1/20,000

MARTINPUICH

POZIERES

Contalmaison Villa

Bazentin-le-Petit Wood

CONTALMAISON

Mametz Wood

The Quadrangle

The Crucifix

Bottom Wood

30.9.16

Capt. R.E.
O.C. 128th (F^d) R.E.

Vol 13

Confidential.

War Diary
of
128th (Field) Company R.E.

from 1st October 1916 to 31st October 1916

(Volume XV)

A de Fonblanque Capt RE
O.C. 128th Fd Coy. R.E.

1-11-16

Army Form C. 2118.

WAR DIARY
or
INTELLIGENCE SUMMARY
(Erase heading not required.)

Instructions regarding War Diaries and Intelligence Summaries are contained in F. S. Regs., Part II. and the Staff Manual respectively. Title Pages will be prepared in manuscript.

Place	Date	Hour	Summary of Events and Information	Remarks and references to Appendices
BECOURT WOOD	1st		Two sections worked in moving on tramway. Remaining section stood by in case they were required. WOs contemplated by in afternoon. Put	
	2nd		Company stood by. Permission obtained to Rest Day.	
	3rd	10 am	3 Sections continued work on ballasting the tramline. 1 section removed Armstrong huts from D.H.Q. West of ALBERT and erected them in SHELTER VALLEY. Put	
	4th		Started work on branch tramline from CONTALMAISON - MARTIN PUICH line about 500 yds running due N. past the Western End of MARTIN PUICH. Continued ballasting tramline. Put	
	5th		Two sections assisted by two sections 102nd Sec Coy RE. continued work on branch tramline. Work slow owing to necessity of making an embankment - & the key cut up nature of the ground. Put	
	6th		Two sections continued work on ballasting. Put	
	7th		3 sections on Branch tramline. 1 section on ballasting. Put	
	8th		4 sections by night working on Gravel tramline - (1 supplying rails, 1 section laying track, remainder working on formation) cannon light night - rest at intervals - satisfactory progress. Put Company stayed to 6.15 to finish work. An officer from 91st Coy Con RE. 152 Div.? arrived to take on work on tramway. 2 Lieut Cope took him on the line - offr. standing over reports attached Put	Appendix I

2449 Wt. W14957/Mgo 750,000 1/16 J.B.C. & A. Forms/C.2118/12.

WAR DIARY
or
INTELLIGENCE SUMMARY

(Erase heading not required.)

Army Form C. 2118.

Place	Date	Hour	Summary of Events and Information	Remarks and references to Appendices
BECOURT WOOD	8th (Oct.)	4.0 p.m.	Orders received from C.R.E. to stand fast in billets pending instructions for a move. Red	
"	9th		Coy. Standing by in billets awaiting orders. Red	
"	10th		" " " " " " Red	
"	11th	6.0 a.m.	Transport left by motor march for VAUCHELLES LES QUESNOY - and billeted at ST SAUVEUR en route. Advanced billetting party under 2/Lieut COPE left by lorry for VAUCHELLES. Red	
"	12th	9.0 a.m.	Advanced billetting party under Lieut ANDREWS left by train for POPERINGHE. The Remainder of the Company left the bivouac at BECOURT WOOD at 3.0 p.m. & marched to the station at ALBERT arrived 7.0 p.m. where it entrained. The transport arrived at VAUCHELLES LES QUESNOY & billeted.	
In train	13th		Company train in train between ALBERT & LONG PRÉ LES CORPS SAINTS. Traffic blocked - men consumed emergency rations. Transport marched from VAUCHELLES to CAULON VILLERS and billeted.	
CAULON VILLERS	14th	3.30 am	Company arrived at LONG PRÉ LES CORPS SAINTS - leaving train 25 kms on the journey. The Company bivouacked then taken by M.T. lorry to CAULON VILLERS and billeted in the village.	

WAR DIARY
or
INTELLIGENCE SUMMARY

(Erase heading not required.)

Army Form C. 2118.

Place	Date	Hour	Summary of Events and Information	Remarks and references to Appendices
CONTEVILLE	15th	6.04 a.m.	Marched to CONTEVILLE & entrained for HOPOUTRE - near POPERINGHE	
POPERINGHE	18th	3.30 a.m.	Arrived at HOPOUTRE & marched via POPERINGHE to HALIFAX CAMP at A.14.c.3.8.9. Tents & huts. Coy	
"	19th		A.E. Coy with Section Officers went round trenches R to L then over from B# (390) Coy. Anchakai Engineers. Took over from FOSSE WAY on 151h to N60 ST. on Left. On 956m. O.C. Coy. meets H.Q. 7th Bde. and arranges for permanent working party of 40 men R to L attached to Coy. for work on mined dug outs on CANADA ST & HEDGE STREET - (Map attached) (See No 7 Sect.) Continuing travel by small parties into YPRES - and took over billets vacated by 6th (Coy) Aust? Eng.rs in RUE de LILLE. No 4 section started work on mined dug outs - Nos 3 + 2 went on work of the class: reinforcement stores carrying parties Rd.	
YPRES	18th		A. Coy went round trenches with C.R.E. + G.O.C. 7th Bde. It was decided to undertake work in the following order of urgency (1) Drainage & revetment of N60 SHAFT HILL ST. and CRAB CRAWL (2) Drainage & VANCOUVER and completion of ST PETERS ST. between WINNIPEG and front line. (3) Drainage, revetment + upkeep of front line & junction of Trees & etc. - (4) Reclamation of WINNIPEG between ST PETERS & CRAB CRAWL.	
	19th		Night parties worked on front line - N60 & CRAB CRAWL.	

WAR DIARY or INTELLIGENCE SUMMARY

Army Form C. 2118.

Place	Date	Hour	Summary of Events and Information	Remarks and references to Appendices
YPRES	20th		Protected Dugouts of Reserve Battalions at the BUND of ZILLEBEKE Lake. Reported their foreward condition to C.R.E. Infantry and R.E. worked on front line, ST PETERS ST – HILL ST & VIGO. Mining of deep dugouts continued day and night in H.Q.1/5. No.1 Section brought up from rest billets for work.	
"	21st		Work continued all day on CRAB CRAWL which has been made passable for 13th reliefs tonight. Drainage of VIGO continued – This trench has a good fall away from the enemy – but is blocked in many places – Firesteps in front line continued by day. Repairs carried out at 13th H.Q. No night work except carrying – owing to Batten reliefs.	
"	22nd		Work on ST PETERS ST. completed. No.2 Section revetting CRAB CRAWL by day – clearing with Infantry by night. – No.1 Section clearing revetting VIGO.	
"	23rd		Work continued 15ft. of damaged trench in WINNIPEG refained.	
"	24th		Work continued – O.C. reconnoitred STAFFORD trench and the BELT – with a view to reclamation throughout.	
"	25th		Work continued – 2 R.E. & Pioneers assisted garrison in draining STAFFORD trench. Watershed OBSERVATORY Ridge road – O.C. reconnoitred STEWART trench with G.O.C. 75th Bde. with a view to reclamation.	
"	26th		Work continued – some repairs made to revetment of CROSS trench – All trenches heavily bombarded to-day with Minenwerfer – 6" – 4.2 and pipsqueaks – considerable damage done.	

2449 Wt. W14957/Mg0 750,000 1/16 J.B.C. & A. Forms/C.2118/12.

Place	Date	Hour	Summary of Events and Information	Remarks and references to Appendices
YPRES	27/8		Work continued - No 3 Section ust Infantry hut in 87 Kans + 3 others today on their hats. Part this is due in bare fact of the excellent exists of having a permanent working party of 225 h.p. mainly tradesmen from each of the three hundred new huts site, under an infantry officer from that work. Reg as work starts to number D daily parties - Off & Staff of two Pioneer started days might work on VANCOUVER Trench & I/watson L₂ working S. From 1160 - & L.N. Lan & PETERS ST.	
	28/8		Work continued - Reclamation of HILL ST. started from BORDER Lane - satisfactory progress everywhere	
	29/8		Work continued - Floor drain put till the east of JG Sapt- to main STEWART ST. out towards the enemy - food trough in STAFFORD ST. Trench-boards straightened in ZILLEBEKE Trench - BQ 2 relief tonight	
	30/8 31st		R.E. floated over by B.H. relief - Box respirators Spell by one tested. Park entrained at 11/110 in hand but taken from Fort Bell - Permanent working parties of 25 men from 2nd J 10th & 11th Bns. North. Fusiliers & 10 men from each of 12th & 13th Bns. Durham L.I. Infantry accommodation in Pound. Work started in ST. Mary's Hostie. YPRES or constring Sund both army's room	

Jas McKenzie Capt R.E.
OC 92K 591 Coy R.E.

Appendix I.

Tramways. Copy Report from
C.R.E. 12th Corps R.E. to C.R.E. 51st Div. R.E.

8-10-16

Tramway.

The tramway from SHELTER VALLEY to
MARTINPUICH has been taken up to a point
M.32.a.5.6 —

A trough line is being laid from about the point
S.16.9.6½ past the W. side of MARTINPUICH and
(at the insistence of 15th Div. Corps) has at base
reached about the point M.31.d.9.4 — The forward
proposed route is shown dotted on the attached
tracing.

Ballast — Most trouble we have is bearing the
loose wet chalk and no opportunity is taken to
tip over the ground and to to strewn were necessary
comes of broken. Two quarries are now in use —
one on the right hand side going up about X.16.c.9.6
& the other on the left hand side about X.10.d.9.5. The
gravel for both lines is to be had — the
position to the N of the main ridge at X.6.c. under
Bank after line —

Where not ballasted with chalk the lines have
been packed with earth, but this gets washed
away in wet weather —

Truck. The C.E. 4th Corps sends truck by lorry
to the point where the line crosses the FRICOURT-
CONTALMAISON road — about X.22.6.1.7. Thence

it is run up by trolley to railhead.

<u>Time for work</u>. At present on the MARTINPUICH ridge it is better to work by night than by day. The ground is very cut up & 2 sections (or 2 platoons p[er] division) are barely enough to keep the formation ahead of the tracklaying party. At least 1 section (or platoon) is wanted for the supply of track, and for laying it out. A few men are required for the actual laying.

Rex Finlason Capt RE
O.C. 1st & 2nd Coy RE

8-10-16 —

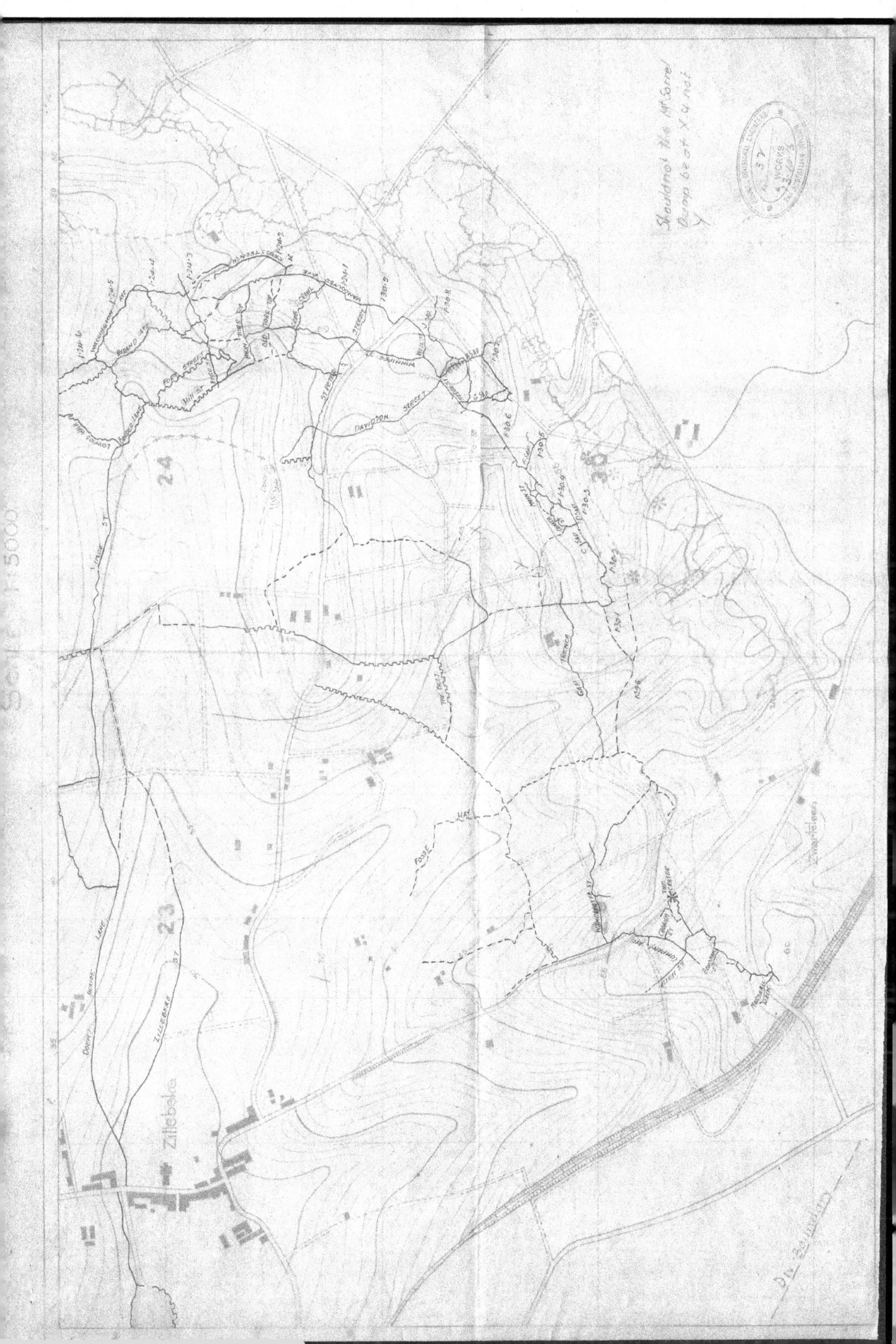

Vol/4

Confidential

War Diary

128th (Field) Company R.E.

from 1st November 1916 to 30th November 1916

(Volume XX)

J. a. Barlowsme
Capt RE
OC 128th Field Coy RE.

Army Form C. 2118.

WAR DIARY
or
INTELLIGENCE SUMMARY
(Erase heading not required.)

Instructions regarding War Diaries and Intelligence Summaries are contained in F. S. Regs., Part II. and the Staff Manual respectively. Title Pages will be prepared in manuscript.

Place	Date	Hour	Summary of Events and Information	Remarks and references to Appendices
YPRES	1st		Work continued as usual. One party started on VANCOUVER & drain dug through hamlet of HANOVER by night.	
	2nd		Work continued. Good progress made by permanent infantry working party on WINNIPEG. Driven ST PETER'S ST. and CRAB CRAWL.	
	3rd		Work continued - STAFFORD Trunk going slowly as we have very hard difficulty in getting up stores.	
	4th		Work continued -	
	5th		Coy. Posted onto BELL RIDGE - Church Parade - Baths & Clothing Inspection.	
	6th		Went round ridges with CRE in connection with Schemes for demolition.	
	7th		Work carried on as usual. Instrumental Dug Outs & Bt Batts with CRE. Continuous ramparts underneath work - Dss? Dug Outs in Hedge St. Loudoun to 2nd Canadian Tunnelling Coy. at midnight.	
	8th		No 4 Section relieved from deep dugouts except Hori a CANADA ST. Pot on relaxation of STAFFORD ST. North of OBSERVATORY Ridge. Work completed on Gun workdrying room in ST MARY'S Hospice - YPRES & Star Post on 2 Gunport - drying rooms in Old Gunpits near Bund - Site chosen for new Aid Post in Bund.	
	9th		Arranged with Garrison to start repairs to dugouts in Bund - Other works usual.	

WAR DIARY or INTELLIGENCE SUMMARY

Army Form C. 2118.

Place	Date	Hour	Summary of Events and Information	Remarks and references to Appendices
YPRES	10th		Box Respirator - Ceremonial. Voluntary Church Parade. Drill with Box Respirators. 1 Platoon Parade continued work in VIGO - E.F.G. Reclamation of VIGO ST. and CRAB CRAWL commence completed.	
	11th		Work continued - Davey's by Staff for a Regt Battalion for extending work towards ST PETERS. Man started on WINNIPEG. Reclamation from CRAB CRAWL for faster - Inten to VANCOUVER working night and left from Junction with CRAB CRAWL. E.F. inspected Battn Gritons near BLAUWE POORT Farm parapets on gunnery. Work as usual. Constructed repairs & damage by Stokes in a Stop Butt.	
	12th		Work as usual.	
	13th 14th 15th		HEDGE ST. & new Butts DAVISON ST. finished for fire trench Scotts - Honour Plank in front of MT SORREL. Other work continues. Chief Engineer Second Army - with CREB, G. So, 2 Bde Div. 2 inspected work on Bonavec front - in particular HILL & VIGO streets - VANCOUVER - to REDAN & STAFFORD ST.	
	16th			
	17th		Bn Relief. 9.0 am. Coy fatigues - 10.0 am. Church Parade (11/3/6) 11.0 am Drill with Box Respirators.	
	18th		Work continued as usual. Ammr galleries totally collapsed in CANADA ST. completed.	
	19th		Work as usual. A mistake Bangalore Torpedo was fired in the afternoon with poor results - at the same time O.C. 2nd Canadian Tunnelling Coy fired a Portable	

WAR DIARY
INTELLIGENCE SUMMARY
(Erase heading not required.)

Army Form C. 2118.

Place	Date	Hour	Summary of Events and Information	Remarks and references to Appendices
YPRES	19th (Cont.)		had mine consisting of 32 lbs of gun cotton in a wooden box. Placed in the centre of a trench as an experiment in blocking or destroying hostile obs — the results were not satisfactory. Woodaney's was done which could not be any equity examined.	
	20th		Work as usual. In the morning Elliot O.Ps. with the assistance of 6 Sappers placed & fired a Bangalore Torpedo to destroy enemy's wire opposite CROSS Trench — on TOP TOP. The object was to cut a lane through the wire for a raiding party. Lengths of torpedo were taken out — the 25ʳ end being electric leads connected — the lengths being pushed through and connected up onto skids. When 22 ft had been pushed through it was found hostile & there was further, it was thought that the lead had reached the enemies parapet immediately after fuse of the mine. After the explosion from E.O.P. the grains remained intact. A large shell crater at the ft of the lane cleared was transfer to front doubt the obstruction. Sub in CROSS BETZE. Sub	
	21st		Work as usual. Reg. Aid Post started where 2WEBEKE Trench crosses the road	
	22nd		Work as usual. Bomb store started in CROSS CRAWL & ST PETERS ST. Bde. Relief — Complain noted — O.C. Work wounded this aft. Capt. 70th Batt. Tunnelers heavily	
	23rd		trench — mortared all day. Much damage done. Sub A.D.S.S./Forms/C. 2118.	

WAR DIARY
or
INTELLIGENCE SUMMARY.
(Erase heading not required.)

Army Form C. 2118.

Place	Date Nov.	Hour	Summary of Events and Information	Remarks and references to Appendices
YPRES	24th		Work as usual. Boant Slits started in CRAB CRAWL. Resumption of communication trench between VANCOUVER and CROSS STREET started.	
"	25th		Work continued in heavy rain. Parapet of Sap 'G' made up with sandbags by night. WINNIPEG being reclaimed. Left of ST. PETERS at fire point Reb.	
"	26th		Work as usual.	
"	27th		Work as usual.	
"	28th		Work as usual. Went round trenches with C.R.E.	
"	29th		Started mining under parapet for new Sap just South of junction of right end of CANADA ST. and Front Line. Started reclamation of Sap at Rear end of VIGO ST. Reb.	
"	30th		Company rested - Fatigues, Church Parade & Pay. Reb.	

P. au Fontangue Capt RE
O.C. 170th (St) Coy RE

Vol 15

Confidential
War Diary
of
128th (Field) Company R.E.
from 1st December 1916 to 31st December 1916
(Volume XVII)

P. de Satgé...... Major R.E.
O.C. 128th (Fd) Coy R.E.

WAR DIARY or INTELLIGENCE SUMMARY

Army Form C. 2118.

Place	Date December	Hour	Summary of Events and Information	Remarks and references to Appendices
YPRES	1st		Work as usual. Good Progress on WINNIPEG - Rd.	
"	2nd		Started work on UT framing VINCE STREET between ZILLEBEKE Lake and ZILLEBEKE Village. Started excavation for 2 Regt. Dressing Stations behind STAFFORD ST. where Sanctuary Dump Road crosses the trench. Lieut. G.V.C. RAWLINS joined the Company as a 2nd in Command from today. 150 Infantry Pioneers are at the disposal of the 2nd Ht. & Coy. in the two systems as follows. Each battalion details 25 picked men to be permanently detailed for work under RE as Pioneers. They remain, so detailed for as much of their time in the line - leaving 5 men per battalion to return the New batch. Said It Coy has the 100 men from the Brigade in its section of Front & 50 men from Bos in reserve. These men live in YPRES.	
"	3rd		Work as usual.	
"	4th		Work as usual.	
"	5th		Work as usual. A shortage of O/Ranco sent out by night left work out of material for work the next day. Taylor arranged for company to start next day. Bn. ¾ left at night.	
"	6th		Coy. & Bn. Baths &c - O.C. with O.C. Ht. Group R.A. selected site for Artillery O.P. at Farm in I.28.b.4.7.	

Army Form C. 2118.

WAR DIARY
or
INTELLIGENCE SUMMARY.
(Erase heading not required.)

Instructions regarding War Diaries and Intelligence Summaries are contained in F. S. Regs., Part II. and the Staff Manual respectively. Title pages will be prepared in manuscript.

Place	Date Dec/15	Hour	Summary of Events and Information	Remarks and references to Appendices.
YPRES	7th		Work started in NEW YORK TO R. Reconnoitred proposed trench joining GAP trench to CANADA ST. under cover of fog. B.E.E. reliefs at night.	Past
"	8th.		Went over whole front with O/C E. Shortages of stores very apparent. Owing to bad damming water on night of 6th + 7th.	Past
"	9th.		Went over Rt. battalion front not able to obtain to this extent trench communications. 22nd Reg. COLLINGWOOD reported Company from leave.	Past
"	10th.		Work as usual.	Past
"	11th.		No 1 Sector Completed WINNIPEG TRENCH from NEW YORK TOP to FORT ST. Reconnoitred Continuation of WULVERIE ST. to Corner of MAPLE COPSE with O.C. No 1 Sector (Lieut Rawlins). Work to be started on 18th.	Past
"	12th.		Company as Yesterday. B. reliefs	Past
"	13th.		STAFFORD ST. Completed to BELT but too thin sticks in places. Work started draining BELT. Considerable artillery activity in Ypres outbreak particularly on WINNIPEG and Communications	Past
"	14th.		Work continued. Right Battalion started in communication trench throughout the day.	Past
"	15th.		Very heavy bombardment of 25th battalion trenches in morning. He trenches

WAR DIARY
or
INTELLIGENCE SUMMARY

Army Form C. 2118.

Place	Date	Hour	Summary of Events and Information	Remarks and references to Appendices
YPRES	15th		Near DEAD END – on extreme right one isolated by to complete destruction of Front Line of about 30 x 40 yds S. of CANADA ST. Another block between N. of LIVING TRENCH & the front line practically isolated the trenches about CANADA ST., WINNIPEG. HEDGE ST. & WELL ST. suffered severely – ST. PETERS and DAVIDSON ST. to a lesser degree but severely. Another attacks bombardment at about 11 a.m. (no accompanies) by an enemy raid on the isolated trenches on the 25th M. – Took up Infantry workers parties of 200 men – with R.E. Recon officers & Sappers to supervise – and Chinese trenches sufficiently to establish communication to the block made evident 30 x North of DEAD END. Road	
	16th		All available men working on repairs. All looks due to bombardment observed except LIVING TRENCH. No further bombardment today. Good progress made. Three portable mine were found on the south at Sap C, apparently brought across by the enemy and nothing noticed flowing in. One mine was there also, but	
	17th		No S. section to or section of attacks pioneers only on repair work due to a from bombardment today. Work forwarded in WINNIPEG.	

2353 Wt. W2544/1454 700,000 5/15 D. D. & L.   A.D.S.S./Forms/C. 2118.

WAR DIARY or INTELLIGENCE SUMMARY.

Army Form C. 2118.

(Erase heading not required.)

Instructions regarding War Diaries and Intelligence Summaries are contained in F. S. Regs., Part II. and the Staff Manual respectively. Title pages will be prepared in manuscript.

Place	Date DEC	Hour	Summary of Events and Information	Remarks and references to Appendices
YPRES	17th		CRAB CRAWL, TOPP TOP, VANCOUVER, VINCE ST, LILLEBEKE ST & STAFFORD ST. 101st & 102 80 R.E. Bath Pde Standard over left Baths over to OC 101st & 102 80 R.E.	
	18		Works to clear HALIFAX ST. Reconnaissance of the trenches through to junction of the BELT. Very too ground & recently No reported during day no apparent change work not so good as last night due to shrapnel being lower & the trenches went as usual	
	19th		Work as usual	
	20th		Heavy bombardment during morning & the return Direct hit on stage L.I.(three) VANCOUVER (three) & WINNIPEG (three) work 25 Sap. Duckboards taken over from the 104 at GAPE. Sky was cloudy between HEDGE ST & ST PETERS repairing VANCOUVER. Baths rebuilt at night	
	21st		Work as usual	
	22nd		Work as usual between 6 & 8 P.M. D went to left company front bombarded went to a carrying party to assist in clearing. All sheds destroyed during night Bridge No 13 slightly damaged by shell fire. Work as usual. Shortage of stores on front line repair work on camps huts. Were dragged for digging, the trenches night 69 to Pole relieved 68 th	
	23rd			

Army Form C. 2118.

WAR DIARY
or
INTELLIGENCE SUMMARY.
(Erase heading not required.)

Instructions regarding War Diaries and Intelligence Summaries are contained in F. S. Regs., Part II. and the Staff Manual respectively. Title pages will be prepared in manuscript.

Place	Date	Hour	Summary of Events and Information	Remarks and references to Appendices
YPRES	24th		Work as usual. Informed Bn 69 & Bde of necessity of clearing away flasks in STAFFORD	
"	25th		sandbags & flagstone lining. She and his sawing flasks in STAFFORD by raid.	
"	26th		Work as usual.	
"	27th		Work as usual. Prolonged bombardment of whole of sector. Gas's Horse STANDS WINNIPEG blocked in two places, otherwise not much damage. 2/Cpl Bell proceeded on leave. Baker returned.	
"	28th		Work as usual. Sum of trenches with C.R.E. & observed position of proposed trench between HALIFAX & STAFFORD. Some shortage of material on most jobs, as no convoys have arrived till to-day.	
"	29th		Work as usual. Sector heavily bombarded during morning. Major Pole Carburque returned from leave etc.	
"	30th		Work as usual. Took our work in progress from Capt. Lockmore. Rev. C.R.E. Camp down to morning. Battalion still in Firing - Rev.	
"	31st			

J. Lockburne Major RE
late Lockburne Major RE
O.C. 178th (H) Coy. RE.

Vol 16

Confidential
War Diary
of
58th (Field) Company R.E.
from January 1st 1917 to January 31st 1917.
(Volume XVIII)

J. A. Potlawson   Major R.E.
O.C. 58th Field Coy R.E.

WAR DIARY
INTELLIGENCE SUMMARY

Army Form C. 2118.

Place: YPRES

Date	Hour	Summary of Events and Information	Remarks
1st		Company at rest. Church Parade. Inspection & baths. Ypres shelled about 5.30pm and 10pm. Ypres heavily bombarded by French mortars in retaliation for activity on B.N. of his Division. Working nearing Ypres destructed to repair damage & other Pests. Pat.	
2nd		Work as usual. No 3 Section in front line almost entirely on repairs. Very little damage done to effect line. Reconnoitred for tunnel to join up STAFFORD to HALIFAX and HALIFAX to DAVIDSON – Pat	
3rd		Work as usual. In the evening laid out from HALIFAX commencement of tunnels towards STAFFORD and DAVIDSON – and from STAFFORD commencement of tunnel towards HALIFAX – Pat	
4th		Work as usual. Excavation started on tunnel from HALIFAX to STAFFORD ST. Pat	
5th 6th		Work as usual. Pat	
		Work as usual. Ypres shelled in the evening from about 5.0pm to 8.0pm. Casualties 2 men wounded – 1 mule killed. Pat	
7th		Work as usual. 2 LILLE BEKE ST. & No 2 MAPLE COPSE Camp flagged with visors notting – Two round butts shelled in afternoon – Certain look out rather tryn. Pat	

Army Form C. 2118.

WAR DIARY
or
INTELLIGENCE SUMMARY.
(Erase heading not required.)

Instructions regarding War Diaries and Intelligence Summaries are contained in F. S. Regs., Part II. and the Staff Manual respectively. Title pages will be prepared in manuscript.

Place	Date Jan'y	Hour	Summary of Events and Information	Remarks and references to Appendices
YPRES	8th		Not as usual. Brigade Relistro at night. Capts. Stanced from learn. Town - Schiding Enhance (Menin + Lille Gates + Sally port) heavily bombarded throughout the afternoon - Both footbridges over moat broken - Pat	
	9th		Conference visited. Canteen Meeting + Pay Parade - Pat	
	10th		Not as usual - Pat	
	11th		Work as usual. Took over block of St Peters St - very badly broken between Winnipeg and Post line. Took some of No2. Section from HALIFAX to work on ST PETER'S ST. Ground too broken to be water - tools will not stand up - Pat	
	12th		Kingston troops arrived. Continual rain - can make to no position on the broken specials at St Peters St. and Winnipeg. Ground too guetsoaked. Trenches flooding badly & their timing tumbles deguts to - Pat	
	13th		Snow & rain - in the afternoon heavy T.M. Bombardment - Winnipeg badly broken in places - During night rain stopped & hard set in - Pat	
	14th		Put boss parties on to St PETER'S St, Winnipeg. Much done in town. Went round with C.R.E. & Issued orders to take over left Bn front to M.s.o - Pat	
	15th		Not as usual - Winnipeg between DAVISON ST and WELL ST obstructed by T.M. fire. Pat	

Army Form C. 2118.

WAR DIARY
or
INTELLIGENCE SUMMARY.
(Erase heading not required.)

Instructions regarding War Diaries and Intelligence Summaries are contained in F. S. Regs., Part II. and the Staff Manual respectively. Title pages will be prepared in manuscript.

Place	Date	Hour	Summary of Events and Information	Remarks and references to Appendices
YPRES	January 16th		Work as usual. Ref	
"	17th		Company went over to Bde slides - Major Ramsay (C.E. 9th ?) arrived on a tour. Church Parade - Inspection of Gas Helmets + Box Respirators - Canteen Mtg. In the afternoon went up to MAPLE COPSE with Major Ramsay & handed over to him the extension of ZUIDERE ST. to STAFFORD ST. & Lt. Lt. 'B' Coy. 9th Staffords. Rel (Raining) Ref	
"	18th		Started work on Communication trench BORDER LANE - HILL ST. - WINNIPEG - WATERTRAP and CRAB CRAWL with No. 1 Section - 2 other working parties and 20 extra attached infantry supplied by 20th Bde. This work was being done by 9th Staffs Regt. (Raining) Ref	
"	~~18th~~ 19th		One tally wounded. Captain Roberts returned from leave. Went Christie went on leave. Went around Ref	
"	20th		Went out line to rear with 9th Bde. burying officer - in front of BEZT. STAFFORD ST & HALIFAX ST. Ref	
"	21st		Proposed westwork from STAFFORD ST & HALIFAX ST, to avenue Ingrant Flanfour & Saffron McKay honoured by shrapnel on MAPLE COPSE checkboards Ref	
"	22nd		Went with Revd. Frinch Norton Officer to arrange for work on T.M. Emplacement in the front system - but the work under of Dhen. Lanks & This Company. Work in A. Br. Area very little. Ref	

WAR DIARY
or
INTELLIGENCE SUMMARY.

(Erase heading not required.)

Army Form C. 2118.

Instructions regarding War Diaries and Intelligence Summaries are contained in F. S. Regs., Part II. and the Staff Manual respectively. Title pages will be prepared in manuscript.

Place	Date	Hour	Summary of Events and Information	Remarks and references to Appendices
YPRES	23rd		Work as usual. Night operation on left Bn. front interfered with work at night.	
	24th		Work as usual. The 20 additional attached infantry making on CRAB CRAWL returned to their battalion. Company worked owing to Bn. Rules/o. Todd. Bde Major 88th Bde came before him.	
	25th			
	26th		O/visit to front. BELT - STAFFORD and HALIFAX ST.	
	27th		Work as usual.	
	28th		CRE. inspected STAFFORD ST. BELT and HALIFAX ST.	
	29th		Work as usual.	
			Work as usual. The front is about 9" in the ground making work very slow. The ground over duck boards may be protected in some extent by covering it with Sandbags regularly.	
	30th		Work as usual - WINNIPEG from CRAB CRAWL to VIGO ST. is now in good order. Work as usual. Visit Christie returning from leave. The front handled satisfactorily from the 13th inst & is still holding.	
	31st			

R. de Fontaine Major R.E.
O.C. 158th (2/1st) Coy R.E.

Vol 17

Confidential

War Diary
of
59th (Field) Company, Royal Engineers
from 1st February 1917 to 28th February 1917.
(Volume XIX)

2/6/17

J. La Fontaine
Major R.E.
O.C. 59th (F.) Coy. R.E.

Army Form C. 2118.

WAR DIARY
or
INTELLIGENCE SUMMARY.
(Erase heading not required.)

Instructions regarding War Diaries and Intelligence Summaries are contained in F. S. Regs., Part II. and the Staff Manual respectively. Title pages will be prepared in manuscript.

Place	Date	Hour	Summary of Events and Information	Remarks and references to Appendices
YPRES	Feb. 1917 1st		Work as usual. Frost still holds - about 9" in the ground - Snowy started to thaw towards evening. Frost throughout the morning afternoon. Coy	Ret
"	2nd		Company sorted army of Brigade Reliefs - Church Roads - Inspections & Canteen Makings.	
"	3rd		Laid out line of New Trench between HALIFAX ST. and DAWSON ST - Bright moon light. Went out to see 23rd Signal Coy - to see site of proposed signal dugout in ZILLEBEKE Bund.	
"	4th		Down to Ridley School to see about O.P. Very hot work in line as usual. Novi 11th F 18 th	Ret
"	5th		Work in line as usual. Frost still holds. Spot dryed with ground. Novi 11th F 18th	Ret
"	6th		Work as usual. Work started clearing DEAD END by day. Work on the BEZT Line now.	
"	7th 8th		Going forward again. Work as usual.	Ret
"	9th		Work as usual. First LEVER wounded between BUND and Billets by shrapnel. Major Rooke visited Coy Hd. on taking over CRE 23rd Division.	Ret
"	10th		Went in line with CRE. dugout front line Pl. B" which had been cleared for wire cutting. Went up - Started from pos. sign - finished today. Bee. Relief. Coy moved - Church house - Refuge Farm & Farm. Both not available owing to Frost.	Ret
"	11th		Work as usual. Slight thaw today - the first that in the frost since 13th Jan.	Ret

Army Form C. 2118.

WAR DIARY
or
INTELLIGENCE SUMMARY.
(Erase heading not required.)

Instructions regarding War Diaries and Intelligence Summaries are contained in F. S. Regs., Part II and the Staff Manual respectively. Title pages will be prepared in manuscript.

Place	Date	Hour	Summary of Events and Information	Remarks and references to Appendices
YPRES	12th		Work started on plans to do short- VIGO ST. and VANOVER - Thaw all set in - Handover work to Capt. A. PODMORE R.E. preparatory to going on course at R.E. School of Instruction.	
do	13th		Work as usual. Major P. du Sarbeaque left for R.E. School of Instruction. Right Battn area heavily bombarded. Much damage to LIVING TRENCH, Lib on front line + HEDGE ST. Both relined	
do	14th		Work as usual. Lt B Bevan + 5 O.R. arrived as reinforcements.	
do	15th		Work as usual. Commenced work on dugouts dug out at the "BUND", also started working on a strong point at DEAD END	
do	16th		Work as usual	
do	17th		— do —	
do	18th		Gas raid. Reconnoitred enemy wire in front of STEWART ST. with a view to making a gap in the morning of the 20th	
do	19th		Work as usual	
do	20		Made a gap in enemy wire in front of STEWART ST. to-day at	

Army Form C. 2118.

WAR DIARY
or
INTELLIGENCE SUMMARY.
(Erase heading not required.)

Instructions regarding War Diaries and Intelligence
Summaries are contained in F. S. Regs., Part II
and the Staff Manual respectively. Title pages
will be prepared in manuscript.

Place	Date	Hour	Summary of Events and Information	Remarks and references to Appendices.
YPRES	20th	3.30 A.M.	by exploding a Bangalore torpedo. 47th Div. reached enemy lines during the night & enemy retaliated on our sector causing some damage	
do	21st		Work on various RE	
do	22nd		Conducted reconnaissance of 225th Coy RE enemy lines & noted also the work on foot with O.C. 225th Coy RE	
do	23rd		Work on various RE	
do	24th		Major P. de Coulanges returned. 2 Lieut S.C. Rawlins. Advance party four 226th Coy RE arrived to take over work & billets. Took no work at Handewin K.T.O. 226th Company RE and marched to Busse Boom where	
"	25th		the Company went into camp. Rest	
"	26th		In camp. Fatigues and fitting marching order. Lecture on forthcoming Training by O.C. Rest	
"	27th		Company marched to HERZEELE went into billets. Rest	
"	28th		Company marched to LEDERZEELE and went into billets. No casualties. Rest	

R. de Coulanges Major RE.

Confidential.

War Diary

of

128th (Bristol) Company R.E.

from 1st March 1917 to 31st March 1917

(Volume XX)

Vol 18

J. A. Fonteneque Major R.E.
O.C. 128th (Bristol) Coy. R.E.

WAR DIARY or INTELLIGENCE SUMMARY

Army Form C. 2118.

Place	Date	Hour	Summary of Events and Information	Remarks and references to Appendices
LEDERZEELE	March 1917 1st	10.30am	Company marched to EPERLECQUES and also with billets to meet S.H. Officer's billets.	
EPERLECQUES	2nd		No ceremonial horse & horses. Rest day. Cleaning wagons, harness, improving billets &c. Rest	
"	3rd		Section training started. Hours 9.30 to 12.45 pm & 2.0 pm to 4.15 pm. Physical Drill. 9.0 a.m. to 12.45 pm. + 2.0 to 4.15 pm. Close order drill. Inspection & cleaning of section individual equipment. Route Marching – Turning – Semaphore &c. Rest	
"	4th 5th		Section training continued. Company drill in afternoon. Rest	
"	6th		Section training. Section officers reconnoitred positions for strong points in connection with Brigade scheme. Rest	
"	7th 8th		4 Strong points dug & 1 look out. Wire being marked out with & without. 4 Sections started out on Brigade scheme. Scheme cancelled owing to weather. Section returned to billets about 2.0 pm.	
"	9th		Section training continued. Lt. A.B. BEVAN left the Company to report to Railway Corps Engineers, ST. OMER.	
"	10th		Section training. No 1 Section demolished lorry tree trunk in parade ground of 8th Hd. in afternoon. Company Drill.	

WAR DIARY or INTELLIGENCE SUMMARY

Army Form C. 2118.

Place	Date March	Hour	Summary of Events and Information	Remarks and references to Appendices
EPERLECQUES	11th		Sunday - Cleaning & other weekly Sanitary arrangements - Church Parade - Lunch into Huts for M. LELOO P. Jones the company. Pat	
"	12th		Nos 1 + 2 Sections - Reached Pontooning & assembling Weldon Trestles on Canal at HOULLE. Divisional Commander inspected work. Nos 3 + 4 Routs March - 4 parties of N.C.O.'s & Sappers from each section set off to find their way to various river crossings at different points of the Company & report on Bridges, demolitions, sector of runs and last a bridge Construction Scheme. Pat	
"	13th		Nos 1 + 2 Pontooning - Nos 3 + 4 Sections - Pat	
"	14th	2 PM	Lectures by Lt R Nos 3 + 4 Sections - Pat Completion of strong Point at EPERLECQUES - Chronical drill musketry instruction - Inspection by M.O. in the afternoon - Pat	
"	15th		Musketry instruction & Chronical drill in the morning. Attacks fired 2 practices on 30x Rifts range in afternoon - Pat	
"	16th		Nos 3 + 4 Sections Pontooning. Nos 1 + 2 Sections route march & reconnaissance Scheme. Pat	
"	17th		Company Sports - Pat	
"	18th		Sunday. Cleaning + other weekly programs - Demonstration of Smoke and Box Mortars - Church Parade - Pat of 89th Inf Brigade - Church Parade - & Inf B.D."	

Army Form C. 2118.

WAR DIARY
or
INTELLIGENCE SUMMARY.
(Erase heading not required.)

Instructions regarding War Diaries and Intelligence Summaries are contained in F. S. Regs., Part II and the Staff Manual respectively. Title pages will be prepared in manuscript.

Place	Date	Hour	Summary of Events and Information	Remarks and references to Appendices
BROXEELE	March 1917 19th		Company moved by march route from EPERLECQUES to BROXEELE & billeted in the villages. No casualties. Lieut Collins proceeded attached to 2nd Army School of Musketry at TILQUES to take charge of Distin's Wakefield ramp gallery. Past	
HERZEELE	20th		Company moved by march route from BROXEELE to HERZEELE and billeted in the vicinity of the village. No casualties. Past	
WINNEZEELE	21st		Company moved by march route from HERZEELE and billeted 2 miles N.W. of WINNEZEELE. Sheet 27. Belgium & France 1/40,000 - Square E25 & E26. Past	
"	22nd		Billet fatigues and cleaning weapons. Past	
"	23rd		No 4 Section - this Cant° moved by lorry to TILQUES - for reorganisation of Rifle Range under 2nd Army School of Musketry. All personnel cicled. Past Coroners drill - Company Drill - &c - Past	
"	24th		Sunday. Church Parade for O.C. Lectures on Strong Points - Coroner drill training.	
"	25th		Day work - Lecture by Section Officers -	
"	26th		Reconnaissance by N.C.O's & officers of RENIN YSER Knivery & nore of Stear No & Section about 20 hrs hard. Past	
"	27th		Inspection Parade by G.O.C. 2nd Army. Lunch & Rendez/vous in WATOU village Past	

2353 Wt. W2544/1454 700,000 5/15 D. D. & L. A.D.S.S. Forms/C. 2118.

WAR DIARY
INTELLIGENCE SUMMARY
(Erase heading not required.)

Army Form C. 2118.

Instructions regarding War Diaries and Intelligence Summaries are contained in F.S. Regs., Part II. and the Staff Manual respectively. Title pages will be prepared in manuscript.

Place	Date	Hour	Summary of Events and Information	Remarks and references to Appendices
HOUVIZETTE	March 1917 29th		Coy. HQrs. 2 Sections had to bathe in tubs in billets, the water being heated in Field Cookers. 1 Section carried out an R.E. reconnaissance. Fine	
"	30th		1 Section bathed — 1 Section Welden Trestle Bridging — One Section Wire & Spars — In afternoon O.C. Coy. gave a lecture at the R.E. Billing School "THIEVES & R.E. Stores — their use & provision". Dull	
"	31st		1 Section WELDON Trestle Bridging — Lecture by M.O. on 1st Aid — Medical Inspection for 1 Section (No map exercise) — 1 Section Use of Prismatic Compass & laying out lines by night. Fog	

J La Fontaine Major R.E.
O.C. 128th Field Coy. R.E.

Vol 19

Confidential.

War Diary
of
128th (Field) Company RE
from 1st April 1917 to 30th April 1917
(Volume XXI)

J. de Fraslauque
Major RE.
O.C. 128th (F) Coy RE

Army Form C. 2118.

WAR DIARY
or
INTELLIGENCE SUMMARY.
(Erase heading not required.)

Instructions regarding War Diaries and Intelligence Summaries are contained in F. S. Regs., Part II. and the Staff Manual respectively. Title pages will be prepared in manuscript.

Place	Date	Hour	Summary of Events and Information	Remarks and references to Appendices
WINNEZEELE	March 1917 1st		No 1st Section - Issolt Rankin & J.C.R., sent by lorry to HOULLE to form No 4 Section under Lieut. COLLINGWOOD - To work on reconstruction of Musketry Range at TIRQUES - Ref	
"	2nd		No 2 Section - Welden Trestle Bridging - No 3 Section Light Infantry bridging - Orders received re Airplane to moor on the 3rd inst. Picked G.S. Wagon & Trestle Wagon in afternoon Ref	
"	3rd		Heavy Snow - Section on cover against shell fire - & Effect of Airplane Ref.	
"	4th		Section Returns on Anti-Gas Precautions - & Gas drill - Laying out trenches & Strong Points - Ref	
"	5th		Company moved to KANORA Camp in OUDERDOM area (M3 central Sheet 28) by march route. Transport in by flat transport. Arrived at 2257 (?) Lieut Christie reports to 225H (?) Coy. i YPRES to take over Mains re. J front line trenches from FOSSE WAY to ST. PETERS ST.	
"	6th		Coy. moved into YPRES after dark - & went into billets. H.Q. at KRUISTRAAT (I.13a 5.3 Sheet 28)	
"	7th		O.C. Coy. with Lients Christie & Cope reconnoitred work in front line - Took over following work - No 2 section: Completion of Tunnel from CANADA Trench to SAP French - Completion of ZILLEBEKE ST. between STAFFORD ST. and the & REDAN - General	

Army Form C. 2118.

WAR DIARY
INTELLIGENCE SUMMARY.
(Erase heading not required.)

Instructions regarding War Diaries and Intelligence Summaries are contained in F.S. Regs., Part II. and the Staff Manual respectively. Title pages will be prepared in manuscript.

Place	Date	Hour	Summary of Events and Information	Remarks and references to Appendices
YPRES	April 1917 7th		Work of Support & Communication trenches in front system - & Supervision of front line work - Nos 2 Section - Repairs & Completion of BELT Trench - Completion of Tramway from VALLEY COTTAGES to BELT - Repairs to OBSERVATORY Trench (from STAFFORD ST. to HALIFAX ST.) - No 1 & 4 Section on establishment. Rob	
"	8th		Nos 2 & 3 Sections commenced work by night - No 3 Section visited our Trenches of DAWSON ST. & HEDGE ST. Hooked by bombardment during the day - Rob	
"	9th		Intense bombardment all day. Culminating in enemy raid about 9.0 p.m. HALIFAX, DAVISON, ZILLEBEKE. STAFFORD and OBSERVATORY Trenches slightly damaged. Nos 2 & 3 Sections [carried?] at midnight & cleared communications. Rob	
"	10th		Work as usual by night. Special working party clearing DAWSON ST - NCO & rifles attached to each of the Companies in the front line to superintend	
"	11th		this work - Rob	
"	12th		Work as usual - At 10p.m T.50 Infantry arrived to be attached for discipline. Rations & work etc.	
"	13th		Day work as usual - No night work owing to Box Respects - Received instructions to take over section from ST PETER'S ST. to MENIN ROAD on night of 15th-16th. Arrangement	
"	14th		2 Sick [illegible] teles over from ST PETER'S ST. to M60 ST. & with 227 Coy RE from M60 ST. to MENIN ROAD. - Rob	

WAR DIARY / INTELLIGENCE SUMMARY

Army Form C. 2118.

Place	Date	Hour	Summary of Events and Information	Remarks and references to Appendices
YPRES	April 1917 15th		Reconnoitred Sector VIGO ST. & MENIN Road with R. 227th Tunl. Coy. RE. - Took over maps of Major Farnham & from O.C. 23rd (F) Coy. R.E. O/C. 227th Tunl. Coy. - Copies of handing over reports to Appendix	*Appendix
"	16th		H.Q. & Officers Mess moved into YPRES - Ruby. Began work in new Sector Started - Bn. Coy. & B.C. "B" Coy. 9th S. Staff.[d] Regt. (Pioneers) work along the N/W long of CANAL west - Excavating & revetting with W/frames - Iuen on "stairs" to road HELL FIRE Corner to ZILLEBEKE - 2 Platoons on deepening & revetting VINCE ST. Post.	
"	17th 18th		Night work on Redoubts started - Copies of allotment of work attached - Went round line with C.R.E. - Arranged to take over northern the Newdemater Trench from the East End of the Promenade PROMENADE - Nearly South of ZILLEBEKE Church and so with the West End of ZILLEBEKE ST - At the same time taken the CRE ordered work on the LILLE GATE Communication Trench to be stopped -	Appendix II
"	19th 20th		Work as usual - Conference with CRE in afternoon - Ordered to give 2 Officers and 13 Coy Pioneers of 162nd Bn Coy in order to assist in urgent work. Management as follows- No 2 Section of this Coy	

Army Form C. 2118.

WAR DIARY
or
INTELLIGENCE SUMMARY.

(Erase heading not required.)

Instructions regarding War Diaries and Intelligence Summaries are contained in F. S. Regs., Part II. and the Staff Manual respectively. Title pages will be prepared in manuscript.

Place	Date	Hour	Summary of Events and Information	Remarks and references to Appendices
YPRES	20th (cont)		No 4 attached Infantry & B Coy. Pioneers. B Coy dispose of 102nd (St.) Coy. This Company to take over the Mount Sorrel Sector from 102nd Coy. B.K. worked by No 3 Section with 2 Sections (50 mm) attached infantry. and 75 mm on a thirty working party from the 75ers Bn. No 4 Section of this company on it 25 attached infantry & such working parties as the B Left Bn can furnish. B Left Bn can furnish. No 1 Section & 25 infantry on ZILLEBEKE Division Road (HOOGE Sector)	
"	21st		Work as usual. Pub	
"	22nd		Bn Relief in Right Sector - Nos 2 & 3 Sectors therefor relied night of 22/23 July Bn Relief in Left Sector - No 1 & 4 Sectors retd. - C.Q.M.S. Daniels & Sergt L.V.J.	
"	23rd		DOHERTY wounded - Lieut Christie & Lt. reconnected sap near DEAD END on MT SORREL. Pub	
"	24th		Visited Bde OC 30th Bge - Work as usual. Pub	
"	25th		Work as usual. Pub	
"	27th		No 2 section with attached Infantry & 2 platoons of Pioneers returned to me from 102nd Coy to which they had been attached - No 2 Section allotted works to tools - Completion of TOR TOP C.T. & of Artillery O.P. to CRAB CRAWL. Heavy Trench Mortar	

Army Form C. 2118.

WAR DIARY
INTELLIGENCE SUMMARY.
(Erase heading not required.)

Place	Date	Hour	Summary of Events and Information	Remarks and references to Appendices
YPRES	27th (cont)		Emplacement at REDAN - Reclamation of MAPLE TRENCH - 1 Platoon Pioneers pals at RUDKIN'S - repair of Fingerboards & camouflage. 1 Platoon Pioneers out some distance & revetting VINCE ST. [signature]	
"	28th		200 Men of 20th London Regt. allotted to this Company for work in HOOGE Sector - Allotted as follows - Assisting Pioneers on VINCE ST. - 20 - 70 men - B². H.Q. HALFWAY HOUSE 10 men - Excavating WEST ST - 10 men, Starting up LEINSTER ST. 40 men Excavating TORR TOP C.T. - 20 men Excavating OXFORD ST along CHINA WALL - 30 men. All the officers in charge of their parties were shewn their work by daylight, & it was arranged with the Battalion that, as far as possible, the same men should do the same work each night. [signature]	
"	29th		Work as usual. Arrangements to move out 20th London Regt. worked very satisfactorily. Orders received to hand over work in progress to 94th (A) Coy. of 18th Div¹. Reconnre Officer of 94th Coy. shewn Tunnel MT. SOERREL & Dugouts.	
"	30th		Reconnre officer of 94th Coy. took over work in HOOGE Subsector - Handing over work made out. Officer 8/94th Bde & O.R.E 2nd Div. Coy Hampton Left Havre last time at 5.0 p.m. for STEENVOORDE. 94th Coy. moved into billets	

Army Form C. 2118.

WAR DIARY
or
INTELLIGENCE SUMMARY.
(Erase heading not required.)

Place	Date	Hour	Summary of Events and Information	Remarks and references to Appendices
YPRES	April 1917	30 F	In YPRES after dark - Dismounted men and attached Infantry of this Coy moved to parade 12-50 am on 1-5-17 for entraining	

R. ac Fatlauspe Major R.E.
P.C. 120 A Coy Coy R.E.

15.4.17.

Handing over Report.
by
2/Lt ——— Coy R.E.

Item	Situation	Nature of Work	Line of Work	Sapper Employed	Infantry Employed	REMARKS
1.	HELL-FIRE CORNER. ZILLEBEKE RD (And HELL FIRE CORNER to NORTH OF ZILLEBEKE DUMP)	Repairing Road. Filling in Shell holes & cleaning road.	About 20% of shell holes filled with brick.	3	8 @ 11-30 P.M.	2 D.A.C. Waggons upset nightly at Say H. Dne at 11-30 & horses to ZILLEBEKE and caused much rumour to vicinity of RATION DUMP. Fell in shell holes. When all holes have been filled in & debris cleared, the road will be metalled.
2.	VINCE STREET	Deepening & running out "U" framed.	250 yds yet to complete.	7, 8, 7	16 @ 5 A.M. 16 @ 11 A.M. 30 @ 9 P.M.	Day & night cont.
3.	CHINA WALL (new alarm OXFORD St.)	Digging new drainage & running out "U" framed.	Completed 250 yds of trench work to entrance towards YPRES.	6	30 @ 5 am	Worked on two sections
4.	RITZ ST. (HALFWAY HOUSE end)	Carrying up to trench lunch. Digging & widening with "U" framed.	"U" framing completed. Some digging & earthing up to do.	5	8 @ 6 am	
5.	WEST ST. from OXFORD ST to LEINSTER ST.)	Digging & running out "U" framed.	"U" framing completed too to yds joining up to OXFORD ST.	8	—	This work is being continued by sappers but trench RITZ ST is employed available. Infantry should assist & complete the work.

Item	Situation	Nature of Work	State of Work	Sappers Employed	Infantry Employed	REMARKS.
6	Batn. Hqrs HALFWAY HOUSE.	Deep Concrete Dug-out with double roof and hidden. (See PLAN attached)	About 65% finished Entrance to be made	9	18 @ 6 am 12 noon 6 P.M.	
7	Signal Dug-out HALFWAY HOUSE.	A Bunch Elephants with two concrete arch, earth cover + hidden	About 75% finished Concrete carrying up & hidden to do.	6	12 @ 6 am 12 noon 6 P.M.	
8	VISUAL STATION for SIGNALS on WEST side of WELLINGTON CRESCENT	A 5'9" hurst dug-out (See PLAN attached)	Not started.	1	1	O.C. Signals has asked for another VISUAL dug-out on EAST side of trench.
9	M.G.E.S WELLINGTON CRES. NORTH	Gallery 5 feet cover to run M.S.E. 20 yds in front of trench behind the line	This is complete & mounting has been fixed.	1	—	Gallery should be kept free of water. Pumping is necessary by Infantry in the line
10	ditto SOUTH.	Gallery 6 feet cover ft 30 feet, then reducing to 14 feet cover and was being extended to west sharps 50 ft further on to the exit.	This gallery has fallen in at the face and will be abandoned. The gallery will be continued with 6ft of cover to the Embrasure and in the exit.	1	M.G. bay of Embrasure The Gallery enters from	Continual pumping is necessary.

Serial	Situation	Nature of Work	State of Work	Sappers Employed	Infantry Employed	REMARKS
11	M.S.E.s RITZ ST NORTH	A gallery 20yds long and 6' of cover to open M.S.E. in east face of trench to fire northward.	Gallery completed & Emplacement framed. Mounting to be fixed.		Christmas Leave from M.G. Coy. & available	Mounting to be supplied by M.G. Coy. We have asked for this. Gallery should be kept free of water.
12	ditto South	A stairway runs down from the trench to a depth of 20 ft. The face is very wet & falls in. It has been abandoned.	Proposed to form a gallery at a depth of 6 ft. to join open emplacement 20yds in front of trench.	1		Continuous pumping is necessary.
	R.E. Material & Dumps					
(a)	Coy DUMP in YPRES I.17.T.0.6.	Load of R.E. Material at this Dump handed over herewith		N.C.O. & 1 PIONEER	1	Only Material kept at this dump needed for urgent repairs to material likely to be required in case of emergency.
(B)	RATION DUMP ZILLEBEKE RD	ditto	See special notes to-day herewith.	N.C.O.	3 for off loading	Infantry are supplied from this Dump nightly from 9pm to 1am.

HANDING OVER REPORT
234 To 128 FIELD Coys RE.

Area from VINCE ST, BORDER LANE HILL ST. VIGO ST exclusive (MAPLE inclusive) to ZILLEBEKE ST & ST PETERS ST exclusive.

WORKS IN PROGRESS.

TRENCHES.

TORR TOP C.T. About 20 yards to be deepened & revetted. Progress slow owing to nature of ground & constant damage by T.M. fire.

MAPLE STREET
Revetting, drainage, fixing of duckboards & construction of Coy H.Q. excavation completed & three section of large elephant erected.

LILLE GATE C.T.
About 200 yards dug 50 yards revetted with "U" frames & panels. Preparation for mining under road made. 25 mining frames complete. 200 "U" frames, 200 revetting panels delivered on site. Bridge to construct over moat at I 14 a 5.1. Trench to be continued between road & railway to I 14 b 9.1.

SALLY PORT No 2 C.T. From I 8 d 3.3. to I 9 c 3.3.
200 yards of trench dug & revetting commenced. 100 "U" frames & panels delivered to entrance of Sally port. Correspondence re this above attached.

PIPE LINE

ZILLEBEKE BUND TO MAPLE COPSE
400 yards of trench dug 1ft wide. 234 feet of 4" pipe screwed & put in trench, left uncovered & camouflaged until tested. Sketch of pipe line & authority for

Pipe Line Coals.
drawing pipes from 3rd R.E. Park attached.

ROADS
ZILLEBEKE ROAD Repair south of I.16.d 7.1
100% ~~85%~~ complete. Shell holes + sides of road being filled up with broken brick.

T.M. EMPLACEMENT.
REDAN Emplacement 85% Complete
Concrete Shelter 50% Complete. Plan herewith.

DEMOLITION SCHEMES
Bridges 12 to 17 inclusive on YPRES–COMMINES CANAL Stores + plans hand over complete.

R.A.M.C.
Aid Post MAPLE COPSE excavation for large elephant dugout complete, Brick for concrete floor carted to site, drain complete.

SIGNAL DUGOUTS
(a) I.22.b.1.2 } Both complete with exception
(b) I.23.a.5.1 } of hurters.

BATHS YPRES INFANTRY BARRACKS 95% complete one canvas partition to fix. plans attached.

O.P's
LOVERS WALK
90% complete parapet to be raised + hurter on top.
TORR TOP 50% complete. passage complete Chamber to be excavated.

ZILLEBEKE DUMP. Hand over with complete list of stores.
9 R.E. truck on siding
MAPS. hand over ZILLEBEKE SECRET 1/10000 2 copies
TRENCH MAP 1/5,000 2 copies
List of Billets area stores etc. attached.
Handed over   Taken over. J. de Fontaine
G. Manley   O.C. 128 Field Coy R.E. Major
O.C. 4th Field Company R.E.

CRE. Appendix II   [stamp: 129TH FIELD COY. No. 54/153 Date 16/4/17 ROYAL ENGINEERS]
23rd Division

Have taken over and attended
work as follows —
TORR TOP C.T. — Completion   ⎫
MAPLE ST — Drainage & revetting &   ⎬ No 2 Section
  construction of Coy. HQ.   ⎪ (Lieut COPE)
T.M. Emplacement REDAN — Completion   ⎬ + 25 a Mx Inf.
A.D.S. MAPLE COPSE   ⎪
O.P.'S — TORR TOP and LOVER'S WALK   ⎭

LILLE GATE C.T. including construction ⎫
 of Bridge to Island and tunnel under ⎬ No 1 Section
 LILLE Road to take TANKS —   ⎪ (Lieut Rawkins)
~~SALLY PORT No 1 C.T.~~   ⎪ + 25 a Mx Inf.
Upkeep of SALLY PORT No 1 Bridge   ⎭

VINCE ST. Deepening & revetting   ⎫ No 3 Section half
  with V frame — Sandbagging &   ⎬ 25 M/ a Mx
  bushing up — about 25.0" masonry⎪ 2 Platoons 'B'
                                  ⎭ Coy Pioneers (less
                                    15 men on T.M. Emp.5)

RITZ ST. — Trench boarding — Sandbagging ⎫
 & bushing up —   ⎪
WEST ST. Short length to be revetted — Whole ⎬ No 4 Section
 to be sandbagged & bushed up —   ⎪ with 25 a Mx
LEINSTER ST. Superintend bushing up   ⎪ Infantry —
 by garrison   ⎪
Bn. HQ. HALF WAY HOUSE — to be completed ⎪
 with double concrete roof   ⎪
Signal Dugout — HALF WAY HOUSE — Complete ⎭

OXFORD ST - Alleyside CHURCH
WALL - MAISON doz - h.h.
continued & GORDON HOUSE.
Work going on in 3 places.

[Stamp: 129TH FIELD COY. ROYAL ENGINEERS No. ... Date ...]

2 Platoons B Coy. 9th S.S.
Pioneers (This 8 men on
roads)

HELL FIRE CORNER - ZILLEBEKE ROAD
Filling in Shell holes with broken brick. Own Pioneers.

2. I propose shortly to start work on two M.G.E's
one in WELLINGTON CRESCENT & 1 in RITZ
Street - which need completion -

3. The following work was taken over but has
not been continued -
    No 2 SALLY PORT C.T. (under your instructions)
    Pipe Line ZILLEBEKE LAKE & MAPLE COPSE (continued
    by Siege Coy.)

4. I should be glad if you would
let me know to what R.A.M.C. unit I should
apply for labour to continue the A.D.S at
MAPLE COPSE -

5. The general condition of the trench system
of trenches is satisfactory -

P. de Fonblanque Major R.E.
O.C. 129th Fd/Coy R.E.

Vol 20

Confidential

War Diary
of
128th Field Company R.E.
from 1st May 1917 to 31st May 1917.

(Volume XXII)

Original

Army Form C. 2118.

WAR DIARY
or
INTELLIGENCE SUMMARY.
(Erase heading not required)

Instructions regarding War Diaries and Intelligence Summaries are contained in F. S. Regs., Part II. and the Staff Manual respectively. Title pages will be prepared in manuscript.

Place	Date	Hour	Summary of Events and Information	Remarks and references to Appendices
YPRES	May 1917 1st	12.30 a.m	Division set when eastwards Infantry marched to YPRES Station then entrained at 2.10 a.m. – Arrived GODEWAERSVELDE 3.30 a.m & marched to STEENVOORDE – arriving 5 a.m. – Breakfasts then carried on to the men found in until dinner at 12.30 p.m. – Chairman arms inspection & billets & Tpns. insp.	Pat
"	2nd		Overhaul of Mills & Equipment beginning weapons wagons	Pat
"	3rd		Inspection by G.O.C. 23rd Division	Pat
"	4th		Box Respirator Drill. No 1 & 2 Sections Rast March	Pat
STEENVOORDE	5th		Maj. Col. Ashworth & Hmen reported to 101st Fd Coy. R.E. for work in X Corps Electro-Motor Section Magazine Fatigue – No 2 Section Rast March – No 3 & 4 Sections Column Fatigue	Pat
"	6th		Sunday – Church Parades & Changing Clothing – 4 Officers and 120 O.R. reported from O.D.B. Base for attachment to this unit.	Pat
"	7th		No 1 Sec Making return stores for Division – No 2 Reconnaissance schemes. No 3 & Section route march. Attached Infantry in Lillers Fatigues. Major de Lousargue R.E. left the Unit for duty with C.E. 2nd Army Corps. Police R.E. took over Bay	St
"	8th		No 1 Sec Return to rifle range Chenowith. No 2 Section Baths. No 3 Sec. wagon Fatigues. No 4 Section Rapwa wiring attached Infantry route march	St

Army Form C. 2118.

WAR DIARY
INTELLIGENCE SUMMARY.
(Erase heading not required.)

Instructions regarding War Diaries and Intelligence Summaries are contained in F.S. Regs., Part II. and the Staff Manual respectively. Title pages will be prepared in manuscript.

Place	Date	Hour	Summary of Events and Information	Remarks and references to Appendices
	May			
STEENVOORDE	9th		Proceeded by march route to reserve billets at OUDERDOM. Took over from 81st Fld Co. R.E. Lt Birdie left before took over work at dump HERSKAN from 101st Field Co. R.E. F.G.C.M. assem. at Coffin J. LAWS promulgate on parade at 9.0 A.M.	
OUDERDOM	10th		No 2 & 3 sections working on dump at HERSKAN. 16 R.E. & 50 attached infantry working at 9 unit dump. Remainder of Coy billets & wagon fatigues. Road, Coy & attached infantry took on two Coys on work at D. unit dump.	
"	11th		Work at D. unit dump. HERSKAN dump completed.	
"	12th		Shelters at KRUISSTRAAT taken over from 81st Coy R.E. comm on two Coys on work at D. unit dump & on shelters at KRUISSTRAAT continued.	
"	13th		Baths to 2 & 3 Coy & tramline now finished. Lt Birdie & 6 O.R. to Boesdyke mining area to lay out assumed Canadian works on [illegible] dug outs (EN1) & civilian horses.	
"	14th		No. 1 sect at HQ BUSSEBOOM. No. 2 section & attached infantry proceeded to YPRES for work under O.C. 102nd Coy R.E. Sid at BUSSEBOOM completed.	

Army Form C. 2118.

WAR DIARY
or
INTELLIGENCE SUMMARY.
(Erase heading not required.)

Instructions regarding War Diaries and Intelligence Summaries are contained in F. S. Regs., Part II. and the Staff Manual respectively. Title pages will be prepared in manuscript.

Place	Date	Hour	Summary of Events and Information	Remarks and references to Appendices
OUDERDOM	May 15		No 1 Co. & attached infantry paraded to YPRES for work under O.C. 1st & 2nd F.R.E. 5 Reinforcements arrived today	
do	16		Completed traffic control shelter on KRUISSTRAAT road. EN1 & commenced hut for the 9 C.C. Centurions worked at WINNIPEG camp. Coldmen on reserve fgs. Ammunition dump. Div EHQ at BUSSEBOOM.	
do	17		Work as usual	
do	18		Work in progress on dug outs EN1, Geo Hut WINNIPEG CAMP, hutt for Irish Horse near HALIFAX CAMP.	
do	19		Work carried on as yesterday. 3 Shelters at D.L.I. took down ammunition.	
do	20		Intelligence reports to duty to C.R.E. 4 Officers & 30 O.R. reported for duty from No 9 R.E. One O.R. reinforcement arrived.	
do	21		Completed Gen hut at WINNIPEG CAMP also hutt for A.P.M. at 4.13.d. 3 O.R. reinforcements arrived.	
do	22		Work as usual. Commenced making bridges for wearers in vicinity of Cox Walk. Reconnoitred track between H.17.c.6.4. & I.13.a.4.6. Laid tile 6 oy today.	

2353 Wt. W3544/1454 700,000 5/15 D. D. & L. A.D.S.S. (Forms)/C. 2118.

Army Form C. 2118.

WAR DIARY or INTELLIGENCE SUMMARY.

(Erase heading not required.)

Place	Date	Hour	Summary of Events and Information	Remarks and references to Appendices
OUDERDOM	May 23		Lt Ghube RE returned from leave areas & reported to OC 102 Field Co RE for duty. Work continued at E.N.I. Dugouts Bowl one & camp stores. Other of Bns completed 14 days to FP & new returned at 9 a.m.	
do	24		Work as usual. Commenced work on huts between H.17 & I.13.	
do	25		Work as usual. E.N.I. almost completed, most of the men have been driven on to making advance H.Q.	
do	26		Completed huts between H.17 & I.13. Other work as usual.	
do	27		H.Q. of BRIGADE SCHOOL progressing satisfactorily. Working parties as usual. Repairing tracks & trimming cage camp. Shells intermittently during night of 27/28th. All ranks in the trenches taking cover from machine until 2 a.m. One casualty only. Man later sent to hospital.	
do	28		Some shells dropped round the camp during the morning. Work as usual.	
do	29		BRIGADE SCHOOL job. Shells during night 28/29th. Reconnected H & 6	

WAR DIARY
or
INTELLIGENCE SUMMARY.

Army Form C. 2118.

Place	Date	Hour	Summary of Events and Information	Remarks and references to Appendices
CHOCQUEAUX	May 29th		Rested with available enemy officers during camp at 10.0 pm & later at 2 am (30th) have hour shelter in trenches at rear of camp. No casualties or damage done.	
do	30		Work as usual. Lit sheds round camp at 9.10 P.M. no damage. ⟨?⟩ had shelter returned, having employed work for 162 R.E. dettice	
do	31st		the vicinity of the camp were shelled rather heavily during the night with 5.9". Work at Bone STORE completed, commenced work on a new track at KRUISSTRAAT.	

Rodmore Major RE.
O/C 136th Field Coy RE.

Confidential. Vol 21

War Diary
of
128th Field Company. R.E.
From 1st June 1917 to 30th June 1917.

(Volume XXIII)

Original.

WAR DIARY or INTELLIGENCE SUMMARY

Army Form C. 2118.

Place	Date	Hour	Summary of Events and Information	Remarks and references to Appendices
OUDERDOM	June 1st	—	Took over Band at Brigade School (2nd Div HQ) Prisoners of War cage HAMERTINGHE. Complete absence of track at KRUISSTRAAT. Some shelling in vicinity of camp again during the night. Detachment of 9th NORTS returned to their battalion.	
do	2nd	—	Took no move. Detachment from 11th Battn. 69th Bde arrived in place of 9th NORTS returned yesterday to Bn HQ at GREENWICH RE admitted to civil ambulance with right hand grade, no shelling now comp[lete]	
do	3rd	—	Detachment of 10th and 11th NF proceeded to YPRES for duty with 10 and 11th Bde B's R.E. & Shores & 1st Section returned from 10 & 11 NF Extra attack on infantry took over duties at DUMP from Common cage continued.	
do	4th	—	Took at BRIGADE SCHOOL & Prisoners cage continued. 1st Section, bath, road control at H16 d 1.1	
do	5th	—	Took as yesterday. Completed shelter for road control at H16 d 1.1. Work continued on advance Div HQ & Prisoners cage. S.O.R. returned from STEENVOORDE	
do	6th	—	do	
do	7th	—	do	
do	8th	—	do	

WAR DIARY
or
INTELLIGENCE SUMMARY.
(Erase heading not required.)

Army Form C. 2118.

Instructions regarding War Diaries and Intelligence Summaries are contained in F. S. Regs., Part II and the Staff Manual respectively. Title pages will be prepared in manuscript.

Place	Date	Hour	Summary of Events and Information	Remarks and references to Appendices
ODERDOM	June 10th		Standing by in billets. 2nd Lt M. Mother reported for duty.	
do	11th		do	
do	12th		do	
ZILLEBEKE	13th		Paraded at 9.30 am & marched to front line real inf. Line the attack. We relieve a Regt. L. attacking in two effort line of left Brigade and at 5 am attacking in this connection to attach enemy. I attempt the Company worked in forward trench 2nd to 3rd line in battle. Capt. J. Welby wounded.	
do		11 am	Marched our forward billets & line to 7:29 & 4th Bde Hqrs. forward parties of 2 am & proceeded to find billets at DICKEBUSCH. Dr. Welby wounded at 9 am. Three men killed & one other wounded. Proceeded to rest huts & bivouacs at DICKEBUSCH.	
DICKEBUSCH	15			
do	16		Company moved from ODERDOM to DICKEBUSCH in camp. Lieut. recey'd Major Laughton at WIJVERNOEK. 2 Lieuts. evening huts at NICMAC camp for Bn HQ	
do	17th		2 Lieuts. evening hutged NICMAC camp. 2 Lieuts. an & Corps rec'd at near ST ELOI. Lt Collingwood proceeded on leave	
do	18		York as usual.	

WAR DIARY
or
INTELLIGENCE SUMMARY.
(Erase heading not required.)

Army Form C. 2118.

Place	Date	Hour	Summary of Events and Information	Remarks and references to Appendices
DICKEBUSCH	19th		Work on I th Corps road & at Rifle Range camp continued. Took down 13 water troughs & re-erected 16 near BRASSERIE, DICKEBUSCH ROAD. Commenced work on Baths at BRASSERIE, DICKEBUSCH ROAD.	
do	20		Work on yesterday work on Corps road delayed as no infantry parties available. Erected two water troughs at H.33.d.9.1.	
do	21st		Work as usual on Baths, XIth Corps road & two water troughs at H.34.c.3. Slingo. Bomb Wright & Duffey wounded, all from enemy air action caused by shell fire on Dickebusho road.	
do	22		Work on XIth Corps road, got connecting rails up dose to shell torn road over Dark at 9 mie HQ & 9 mile Baths to one side of ORE	
? Lette	23		No 1, 2, 4 detachmt with HQ & transport transferred to Bus? of the shed at H.3a.3.6. to 3 section remains at DICKEBUSCH to carry on work on XIth Corps road.	
do	24		Cdg of detachmt & shells Poelgers?	

Army Form C. 2118.

WAR DIARY
or
INTELLIGENCE SUMMARY.
(Erase heading not required.)

Instructions regarding War Diaries and Intelligence Summaries are contained in F. S. Regs., Part II. and the Staff Manual respectively. Title pages will be prepared in manuscript.

Place	Date	Hour	Summary of Events and Information	Remarks and references to Appendices
Lebbe	25th June		Dismissed three also. Company sent two pings in "Lone pines right cliff" close	
do	26th		Cleaning out equipment. R.	
do	27th		Dangers & dunes during morning. Efforts & carried off work evening. Shelter A & Runway was erected on the & lock road for clearing the trenches. R.	
do	28th		2/Lt Lokes reports to take over work from 2/Lt Watto. Moved to DICKEBUSCH Boy paraded 6 AM & marched to DICKEBUSCH.	
DICKEBUSCH	29th		2/Lt Watts & 6.O.P.E. SPOIL BANK dug out. 9 men & Went over the at 4 am. There is not a single trench in the sector without at least a foot of mud & water in the bottom. No 2 section working on SPOIL BANK dug outs. No 3 section cleaning IMAGE ROW. No 4 section digging new CoP at 76 attached infantry reports for duty from 76 & 2nd Bn Bedf. K.L.R.	
SPOIL BANK	30th		Line 76 attached infantry returned from leave Lt Collingwood	

Redmore Major R.E.
OC 179th Tun. Coy. R.E.

Sends/... A

Herewith War Diary
of 128th Field Coy R.E.
for month of July 14.

Please acknowledge.

M. Alexander
Lieut R.E.
Adjt R.E.
23rd Division

HEADQUARTERS,
23RD
DIVL. ENGINEERS.
No. A.P.44
Date 5.8.14

Confidential.

War Diary
of
128th Field Company R.E.
1st July to 31st July 1917.

Volume XXIV

WAR DIARY or INTELLIGENCE SUMMARY

Army Form C. 2118.

Place	Date	Hour	Summary of Events and Information	Remarks references Appendices
SPOIL BANK	July 1st		No 3 Section working on 1st Cap. road. No 2 & 4 Section with attached infantry & working party digging no support line behind. RIGHT BATTALION front. No 1 Section on LEFT BATTN communication trench. IMAGE ROW. Corp. G SIMMONS, L/Cpl M. O'POOL & SAPPR HOOTON killed. Sappers F WILLIAMS, O FLANAGAN & T. HADDON wounded. Sapper T. N. SMITH reported missing since moved to HOODCOTE HOUSE AMBULANCE.	
do	2nd		Work as yesterday.	
LARCH WOOD	3rd		Work as yesterday. Moved forward billets from SPOIL BANK to LARCH WOOD dugouts. Sapper FINNIGAN killed. Right Battalion area taken over by No 13 Section.	
do	4th		No 3 Section working on 2nd Corps road. No 1 Section working wit attached infantry & working party on IMAGE ROW. No 2, 1/7, & attached infantry? Working party on IMMEDIATE SUPPORT and CENTRAL AVENUE. Supervised connecting front line posts from I.30.6.64 to I.30.6.61.	
do	5/2		No 1, 2 & 4 Sections & attached infantry working on Sap H. Lieut Collingwood supervised digging front line from I.30.d. 75.90 to I.30.d. 40.30. Work on 2 Corps Road started on 2¼ Scipe Ray Road - No 3 Section working on billets at DICKEBUSCH. Started R.A.P. behind CANADA ST. R.E.	
	6th		No 1 Section Gallacks in Party with Working parts working on IMAGE ROW and Sap F on trench (I.30.6.35.00. to I.30.a 70.90.) Attached infantry working	

A 5834 Wt. W4973/M687 750,000 8/16 D. D. & L. Ltd. Forms/C.2118/13

WAR DIARY
or
INTELLIGENCE SUMMARY.

(Erase heading not required.)

Army Form C. 2118.

Instructions regarding War Diaries and Intelligence Summaries are contained in F.S. Regs., Part II. and the Staff Manual respectively. Title pages will be prepared in manuscript.

Place	Date	Hour	Summary of Events and Information	Remarks and references to Appendices
LARCH WOOD	Continued 6th		No 1 Section working on Tap F. No 2 section working on Tap M. Tres Front line dug from I.30d/7.5c.0.16. I.30.6.85.20. Infant Lorenz wounded (slightly). R.T.C.	
"	7th		Major Podmore & the Adj Capt wounded about 1.0pm out character. Captain Christie assume Command of Coy. Work on yesterday. New FRONT LINE dug connecting up points Shir.Ham.Topo.J.I.30.6.85.70. I.LEAD O.N. — I.30.6.85.20. Shiel.Ham.6.9.10 0R fm 10.1/slightly attacked	
"	8th		FRONT LINE handed over to Brigade for improvement. Obtained work on 2/k/c from night. Heavy rain during morning held up Tunnelly Vy ob Grenade Store in HEDGE d1 and HERMITAGE WOOD DUMP of Tunnelst Lieut Collinson Take charge of Transport Park.	
"	9th		Collecting & carrying stores for Brigade Wood dump - O.Katmin Reports on W.D. 9/10. No 2 section in field safely return No 1 section with Ist co's 9.0 half to DICKEBUSCH. R.T.C.	
"	10th		Working on Park. no 2s R.T.C.	
"	11th			
"	12th		Working as yesterday. Heavily shelled early. Stoker (MARCUS 11 army) Stoker R.T.C. slightly wounded - Lieut. Cope C.E. when from trench. R.T.C. not a return. No 2 section. No 2 section attached to No 1 section & partly returns by No 1 section is safety. R.T.C.	
"	13th		Work on trench Salient HATTS wounded (slight). Sto Nott accidentally injured. Lieut Collingwood evacuated to C.C.S. (sick) Lieut Cope taken charge of train from Park. R.T.C.	

Army Form C. 2118.

WAR DIARY
or
INTELLIGENCE SUMMARY.
(Erase heading not required.)

Instructions regarding War Diaries and Intelligence Summaries are contained in F. S. Regs., Part II. and the Staff Manual respectively. Title pages will be prepared in manuscript.

Place	Date	Hour	Summary of Events and Information	Remarks and references to Appendices
LARCH WOOD	July 14th		2nd Lieut ALLAN R.E. (101st Fd Coy R.E.) & 10 O.R. attached from in place of 2nd Lt HAMILTON & 10 O.R. who rejoin their Coy - 2nd Lt HINTON R.E. from H.Q. Company to Coy in temporary command of No 2 section in place of 2nd Lt. Heath R.E. No 4 section to attack K/38/c, entered by No 2 section & rather in the rear. Capt. HURBY M.C. R.E. arrived at Kemmel on him & took command of Coy.	
"	15th		Work as before. IMAGE SUPPORT barely cleared - Capt RUBY arrived, Command of Coy taken by him (LORENWOOD). Heavy shelling at night Rfc	
"	16th		Work as before. No task hrs I.30.d. 96.06 to I.30.6. 90.70 laid out as shown. Inability to carry fuzes of sand & gravel, whilst carrying gas grenade in respirators of old front line system (MOUNT SOREL) stated by Ryde (Early Ammn). No work at night due to stores being of nature.	
"	17th 18th		No 3 section & Attacks rifts released by No 2 section in No 4 sec. Work as previous. New task I.30.d. 8595 to I.30.6. 6040. (Rear off.	
"	19th 20th		Work as yesterday. No 2 section returns to SICKLEBIRCH & pull of officer & 20 O.R. from 104th Fd Coy R.E. arrive to take on work - Lieut R.G. COLLINGWOOD R.E. commanding. Military Cross.	

Army Form C. 2118.

WAR DIARY
or
INTELLIGENCE SUMMARY.
(Erase heading not required.)

Instructions regarding War Diaries and Intelligence Summaries are contained in F. S. Regs., Part II. and the Staff Manual respectively. Title pages will be prepared in manuscript.

Place	Date	Hour	Summary of Events and Information	Remarks and references to Appendices
DICKEBUSH	21/7		Work handed over to 104th Fd Coy 24th Divn & coy returned to billets at DICKEBUSH in the morning after work. neighbourhood shelled with long range guns during afternoon & night.	MWL
	22/7.		Coy moved to billets at X.10.6.6.8 or METEREN starting 6.0 am. Did not arrive till 5 p.m. owing to our proper billets being occupied by R.A. Capt CHRISTIE went on leave.	Sheet 27.
	23/7.		Cleaning up equipment, wagons, & etc Resting	MWL
	24/7		Two hours training a day, consisting chiefly of drill inspections gas drill, musketry etc. Work interfered with by weather Health of Coy good.	MWL
	25/7			MWL
	26/7			MWL
	27/7			
	28/7.			
	29/7		Sunday Church Parade & sports postponed owing to weather 1810 WILSON admitted to 169th Fd Amb. Sick	MWL

2353 Wt. W2544/1454 700,000 5/15 D. D. & L. A.D.S.S. Forms/C. 2118.

Army Form C. 2118.

WAR DIARY
or
INTELLIGENCE SUMMARY.
(Erase heading not required.)

Instructions regarding War Diaries and Intelligence Summaries are contained in F.S. Regs., Part II. and the Staff Manual respectively. Title pages will be prepared in manuscript.

Place	Date	Hour	Summary of Events and Information	Remarks and references to Appendices
X10 6.6. (FONTAINE HOUCK)	30/7		No I & II Sections carried out a scheme for R A Bridges across METEREN Becque. No III section erecting jumps for Bde Sports. No IV - repairing range at X10C & R33a. Training of Junior N.C.Os & signallers.	
	31/7		Training in morning. Coy Sports held in afternoon. Band of 69th F.A. tent by O.C. & good entries for events. Went off well in the evening of closed down. Rain came on in the proceedings. 2nd Lt. A.L. WILSON returned from F.A. 2 Lt W.M. HAMES went on leave to England.	

Vol 23

CONFIDENTIAL

War Diary
of
128th Field Co. R.E.
Aug 1st - Aug. 31st 1917.

WAR DIARY
INTELLIGENCE SUMMARY
(Erase heading not required.)

Army Form C. 2118.

Place	Date	Hour	Summary of Events and Information	Remarks and references to Appendices
X16 6 81 (FONTAINE HOUCK)	1/8 2/8 3/8 4/8		4 hours Training a day but greatly interfered with by weather. Subjects dealt with :- Drill, solemes, Musketry, Map Reading, & use of compass gas Drill, Signalling, Knots & Lashing, NORTON tube, Well. Certain amount of work done on watts Ranges	Capt Clarke returned from leave etc.
"	5/8		Church parade attended by dismounted men P.E.C.	
ARQUES	6/8		Company moved to ARQUES. the transport by road, the dismounted portion of Company by train from CAESTRE (cyclists with transport). Company forms part of 69th Inf Bde Camp for the purpose of this move. P.E.C.	
HAUT LOQUIN	7/8		Marched as a Company to HAUT LOQUIN, arriving at 9-45 P.M. and moved into billets arranged by advance party. Orders received to Company to move to 18th Corps area for rest in forward zone. P.E.C.	
No 1 POPERINGHE - VLAMERTINGHE Road 29/C.6.a.57	8/8		Left HAUT LOQUIN at 10.0 A.M. — dismounted men by Bus convey direct to transport lines North of POPERINGHE – VLAMATINGHE Road (C.6.a.57 sheet 28). Transport by road to NOORD PEENE (near CASSEL) Cyclists moved to CASSEL where they remained to tonight. P.E.C.	

WAR DIARY or INTELLIGENCE SUMMARY

Army Form C. 2118.

Place	Date	Hour	Summary of Events and Information	Remarks and references to Appendices
28/H.10.6.25 (VLAMERTINGHE)	August 9th		Diamonds men commenced work on forward road, afternoon returning to camp, preceded by 10.17.5.10 by Pt. N/NE of VLAMERTINGHE – YPRES road (H.10.6.25.) where cyclists joined them – Transport rested at NOORD PEENE. R.E.	
"	10th		Transport moved by road to them at G.6.a.5.7. – Diamonds to new works on forward roads – as follows:– BOUNDARY ROAD, H.C.26.6.6.4. to C.21.C.3.4. (Sheet 20.) improving by filling in shell holes and draining. R.E.	
"	11th		Work as yesterday – Sapper TURBA. R. killed. R.E.	
"	12th		Work as yesterday – Sapper COOK.G. killed. Sapper RABBAGE.E. ALDERMAN and MILLER wounded while returning from work – 1 N.C.O. with cement arriving Reg.	
"	13th		Work as yesterday – Some shells fell near forward billets – R.E.	
"	14th		Work as yesterday – 2/Lt. Brig.R.E. evacuated sick – Sappers Fox and BIRD wounded (the latter remaining on duty). R.E.	
28/G.G.a.5.7.	15th		Work in yesterday (in Morning). Forward billets were heavily shelled in the afternoon and had to be evacuated. 2/Lieut Hann wounded in the foot –	

Army Form C. 2118.

WAR DIARY
or
INTELLIGENCE SUMMARY.
(Erase heading not required.)

Instructions regarding War Diaries and Intelligence Summaries are contained in F.S. Regs., Part II and the Staff Manual respectively. Title pages will be prepared in manuscript.

Place	Date	Hour	Summary of Events and Information	Remarks and references to Appendices
G.G.S.7.	August 15th (Continued)		Selected site for new camp 500x west which was shelled a few minutes moving in and length WRIGHT N. wounded. The 4 sections returned to Horse lines for the night. PLC.	
"	16th		(Zero day for 48th Div offensive). No 3 section with limit COLLINGWOOD opened up ADMIRAL'S ROAD and made it passable for horse traffic. No 1, 2 and 4 section made new camp at H.S.A.A. where they rendered PLC	
"	17th		No 1,2 & 4 section worked on ADMIRAL ROAD (improv'g) - No 3 section worked at maintenance until 4.0 pm when they moved up and relieved No 4 section at forward billet. No 4 section returned to horse lines GREENFIELD wounded. PLC.	
"	18th		ADMIRAL'S ROAD continued by forward sections. Afternoon no 1 & 4 section relieve each other. PLC.	
"	19th		Work on maintenance by forward sections. Afternoon No 2 section could not be relieved owing to heavy shelling, No 1 Sapper STEVENSON (cyclist orderly) reported missing. PLC.	

WAR DIARY
or
INTELLIGENCE SUMMARY
(Erase heading not required.)

Army Form C. 2118.

Instructions regarding War Diaries and Intelligence Summaries are contained in F.S. Regs., Part II and the Staff Manual respectively. Title pages will be prepared in manuscript.

Place	Date	Hour	Summary of Events and Information	Remarks and references to Appendices
28/G.6.a.57.	August 20th		No 1, 3 & 4 Section worked for part of time on ADMIRAL'S ROAD. Afternoon returning to trenches — Work and found billets taken over by 101st Fld Coy. R.E. R.L.L.	
"	21st		No 2 section worked in XVIII Corps workshops — Remainder inspection of Iron Rations etc and improvements to Camp. R.L.L.	
"	22nd		No 2 section worked in XVIII Corps workshops — Remainder in Camp improvement. R.L.L.	
"	23rd		No 3 section worked in XVIII Corps workshops — Remain in Camp improvement. R.L.L.	
"	24th		As yesterday. R.L.L.	
"	25th		Camp fatigues in morning. Alarm parties in afternoon. Three 50B's 71a Coy R.E. arrive preparatory to taking over camp. Company turned out took over billets and work from 62nd 71a Coy (4th Bn.)	
CAFE BELGE 2 GA 23/H.30.a.29.			Transport at BICKERBURN H.B.3.6.55 Remainder at H.30.a.29. Party of Officers and NCO's take over work in the lines R.L.L.	

WAR DIARY
INTELLIGENCE SUMMARY

Army Form C. 2118.

Place	Date	Hour	Summary of Events and Information	Remarks and references to Appendices
Cap E BERGS 27. H.30.a.2.9	August 27.		No 2 Section worked on Mule Track around S. of HOOGE CRATER. No 1 Section minor work of strongpoint at GLENCORSE WOOD R.E.L.	
"	28th		No 3 & 4 Section assisted by men of "A" Coy 9th S. Staff (Reserve) worked on Mule Track S. of CRATER and a duckboard track from MENINROAD. No 1 CRATER Board CHATEAU WOOD 3 men left to rest & provision. In ...? J.P. Started yesterday M. 1.2 heights. Working camp held 300 infantry camp was baptised at J.13.a.68 and I.13.6.04. No 1 & 2 section worked sumelles on track in shown above. No 3 & 4 Section made R.E.L.	
"	29th			
"	30th		No. 3 & 4 section working as before - Also No 1 Advance dressing station at J.13.a.24 and car loading point at I.18.a.5.6. Hand stations at J.13.b.25 and J.13.b.95.3. Infantry track 150x and J. of HOOGE CRATER and Advance Dressing station at the ECOLE (YPRES) R.E.L.	
"	31st.		Work on experience on these by 1 & 2 sections. A hand dropped from hostile aeroplane on horse lines at about 2.30 P.M. Causes 21 casualties to horses & mules. 25 horses & mules were also wounded, 8 of which were subsequently destroyed - much damage was also caused to the harness R.E.L.	Ref R.E. — Passing report of services & reinforcements in /6 commenced in /2 ... Jany /5

To accompany War Diary
Aug 1917

Progress Report of Work done by 128th Fd Coy R.E. & A Coy 9th South Staffs since coming into the Line on 26.8.17.

I. HOOGE Crater. Mule Track close to Lip
Picketed with guide Posts
140ˣ improved & corduroyed roughly
Notice Boarded

II. HOOGE crater Infantry Track at 150ˣ distance
Whole Improved for 200 yards.
Posted throughout
Notice Boarded

III. Trench Board Track to CHATEAU WOOD
200ˣ Laid to CHATEAU Wood
200ˣ Doubled
Track through CHATEAU Wood improved.
Track to beginning of trench boards improved & posted.

IV. Advanced Dressing Station at J 13 a 2.4
Repairs 75% completed.

V. Car Loading Point at I 18 a 5.6

VI. Advanced Dressing Station École YPRES
60% Completed.

VII. Water Points (200 Cans)

Established at J13a.4.8.
" on MENIN Road about J13a.4.4

VIII. R.E. Dumps.

Established at J13a.6.8.
at J13b.0.4
+ 95% filled.

IX. Visual Stations

Completed 75% at J13b.2.5.
80% at J13a.80.30.

X. Mule Track HALFWAY HOUSE – ZOUAVE WOOD – MENIN Road.

Completed for mules to I18c.5.8 (about)
Posted through to MENIN Road
Notice Boarded

M Luby
Major R.E.
31-8-17. O.C. 128th 2/L Coy R.E

Confidential

Vol 24

128th Field Co. R.E.

War Diary for September 1917

Vol. XXVI

WAR DIARY or INTELLIGENCE SUMMARY

Army Form C. 2118.

Place	Date	Hour	Summary of Events and Information	Remarks and references to Appendices
Sept [Kendrew]	14		Written before on Trench Board & Hack Tank sent HODGE CRATER 12 men from 102nd Fld. Coy R.E. attacks to Hoonto Lectn. to the R.E. place of annother as rewind Yesterday. Alive knew not much killed yesterday are [thinned] & [hum]. No horse and 2 [such] men [seem] from [recoound depth]. R.E.	
"		2.20	Company [Sto] [by] a killed [or] noon after returning from an E. Two men knew there drawn from [Remound rgmt] [Korea] & [men] were [pains] of men and attacks to [begin]. Throughout to right there one most [touching] from hostile aircraft among [considerable] damage to [appear] done there ([cloistered] [mots]). Shells also fell near the home [bins] at intervals during the night. R.E.	
"		3.10	Notify [rearby] buried Twelve [suffer] four the forward killed [reply line] Three attacks to the Hoonto Section from 102 to the E. Pt. to the afternoon began are facies preparatory to [morning], at send the men are [moved] from [stockerswell] to [suitmans] [pulgmd] [line] Near C.A.P.& 1302.& E. where the enemy [banks] by [Langsan] R.E.	

WAR DIARY
or
INTELLIGENCE SUMMARY

Army Form C. 2118.

Place	Date	Hour	Summary of Events and Information	Remarks and references to Appendices
X.10.C.5.A. (FONTAIN- -HOUCK)	September 1916 4th		At dawn H.E. team for head quarters rags returned to train him no stretchers. Company leave for FONTAINHOUCK (near METEREN) by sections starting at 5.15 A.M. No Q= transport had at horse lines no 8.50 A.M. Arriving at new billets about 12.45 P.M. R.E.E.	
"	5th		The Company had the use of the baths at LABEOUGE FARM during morning. 2/Lieut Watts R.E. and 3 O.R. proceeded to H.Q. 68th Batt for the purpose of laying out practice trenches. R.E.E.	
"	6th		Company employed on fatigue during morning. Marching order kit inspected. R.E.E.	
"	7th		4 hours training - Antigas precautions, care over drill wiring and use of compass.	
"	8th		Training as yesterday. 2/Lt Wilson R.E. sent to report on danger in the front line sap km. 9 to lie in RAILWAY DUGOUT while engaged in the work. R.E.E.	
"	9th		Church parade attended by the sappers - Cricket match div. R.E. versus 9th S.Staffs in the afternoon the former winning. 2/Lt Wilson returned. R.E.E.	
"	10th		No. 2 section reports to establish hyp. bricks Canteen was machine range line billets R.E.E.	

Army Form C. 2118.

WAR DIARY
or
INTELLIGENCE SUMMARY.
(Erase heading not required.)

Instructions regarding War Diaries and Intelligence Summaries are contained in F. S. Regs., Part II. and the Staff Manual respectively. Title pages will be prepared in manuscript.

Place	Date	Hour	Summary of Events and Information	Remarks and references to Appendices
X10C 3A September (FONTAIN NERf)	11th		4 hour kinesis for No 31st section machining Night Rum ok'd by Compan visit Gaselinck in. Mounted Ypres write 10 + 2 PM by in the afternoon - RLL	
"	12th		No 1 + 2 section await inhabitants Difficulties. 3rd relief kinds in at pm. 2/Lt Watts reports for duty to 3rd Bn mod. RLL	
RENINGHURST	13th		The Company moved to ONTARIO CAMP RENINGHURST. RLL	
DICKEBUSCH	14th		The Company Rovers to BURGOMASTER'S FARM, DICKEBUSCH, in trenches 1 + 2 section moved to RAILWAY DUGOUTS. RLL	
"	15th		Formed section works on Dressing Station at J. 19. a. 61. Forward RE Dump at S.D. central and J. 19. a. 07. Collecting station VERBRANDEN RD and Duckboard track to TOR TOP. (from MALET COTTAGES). Back tee line in Infantry, in duck track from DICKEBUSCH to TOR TOP. 90 infantry from 68 I.I/380 attacked Company. RLL	
"	16th		Wink on yesterday formed dumps complete. Dressing Station and TORTOP and Visual signal station at J. 19. 6.13 started. H.Q. Krumport + tank section move Billets to H. 34. a.45. Camp Wrecks B. 10 & 268 by Pts. RLL	
"	17th		Collecting station Dressing station (TORTOP) + Verical signal station complete. 2 bootie points made at J. 15. a. 50 + J. 19. a. 5A. Water found putting in trunk industries 224	

Army Form C. 2118.

WAR DIARY
or
INTELLIGENCE SUMMARY
(Erase heading not required.)

Instructions regarding War Diaries and Intelligence Summaries are contained in F. S. Regs., Part II. and the Staff Manual respectively. Title pages will be prepared in manuscript.

Place	Date	Hour	Summary of Events and Information	Remarks and references to Appendices
DICKEBUSCH	September 18th		All work in hand completed. No 1 & 2 section return to Camp at DICKEBUSCH after work. R&C.	
"	19th		All section inspected individually. All sections inspected in Battle order and allotted tasks for offensive, etc. Moves up to Advanced Brig H.Q. in the evening. No 2 section moves to forward position assembling in CENTRAL DUGOUT (Near A.T.13c N.W.) at dusk. R&C.	Zero 1 day for 2nd Army offensive
"	20th		Nos 3 & 4 section and attached infantry left at 5.30 a.m. and assembled in RAILWAY DUGOUT. No 2 section left early & point at 8.0.10. Traffic first objective had been taken.) + successfully bridges BULBARTON LAKE in several places. Late a small party under command of Lts BRANSVILLE & BEAL (Lts MATHEWSON and PERCIVAL were killed. Lt DUNCAN killed later relieving No 3rd section left assembly point at for the construction of strong points BY D respectively. Delay caused by enemy trench opposite in the right immediately in front of KECKMENDY. When it was found No 2 section returns to DICKEBUSCH for breakfast remainder to R.W.WAY DUGOUTS. R&C.	Zero 5.40 AM. 1st day
"	21st		Nos 3 & 4 section infantry rested. No 1 section Engineer Park, W.W. stores inspection checked equipment. R&C.	

A.S.34 Wt. W.4973/M687 750,000 8/16 D. D. & L. Ltd. Forms/C.2118/13.

WAR DIARY
or
INTELLIGENCE SUMMARY.
(Erase heading not required.)

Army Form C. 2118.

Place	Date	Hour	Summary of Events and Information	Remarks and references to Appendices
DICKEBUSCH	September 22nd		All sections & attached infantry engaged in forming forward R.E. Dumps and in improving tracks & VIII Ride.	
"	23rd		Work on repairing forward dumps, dug-outs, approach & rest tracks & attacked tanks returning to camps at DICKEBUSCH. Approved party from 228 & 710 Coy R.E. took over rest.	
H.32.d.4.2. (WESTOUTRE)	24th		Major Leahy went on leave to U.K. Company moved to WESTOUTRE H.33.d.4.2. Bill. Came under authority of C.R.E. X Corps. Worked on billets. Bill.	
"	25th		Worked on camps, repairs WESTOUTRE area. Bill.	
"	26th		ditto	
"	27th		ditto	
"	28th		Lt. Watts went on leave to U.K. Bill.	
"	29th		ditto and on water trough. Bill.	
"	30th		Company rested. Church parade attended by captain. Bill.	

128th Field Co. R.E.

War Diary for
October. 1917

Vol. XXVII

Army Form C. 2118.

WAR DIARY
or
INTELLIGENCE SUMMARY.
(Erase heading not required.)

Instructions regarding War Diaries and Intelligence Summaries are contained in F. S. Regs., Part II. and the Staff Manual respectively. Title pages will be prepared in manuscript.

128TH FIELD COY. ROYAL ENGINEERS

Place	Date	Hour	Summary of Events and Information	Remarks and references to Appendices
H.32.d.4.2. (WESTOUTRE)	OCTOBER 1st		Worked on camps and water troughs in WESTOUTRE area. Eft.	
	2nd		ditto	
	3rd		Nos 3 & 4 Secs worked on camps & water troughs, Nos 1 & 2 Sec moved to (BERTHEN) R.27.a.3.8.	
	4th		Nos 3 & 4 Sec worked on camps & water troughs and 1 & 2 Secs worked on camps R.27.a.3.8 (Xth CORPS Rough Camp - 23rd Divn Camp)	
	5th		ditto	
	6th		ditto	
	7th		ditto	
	8th		ditto	
	9th		ditto (Major Jenks R.E. returned from leave.)	
	10th		ditto	
H.36.d.2.1/4.	11th		The Company ceased to work under C.R.E. Xth CORPS. The Company moved to H.36 d.4 (Sheet 28) and took over work in the line from 95th Fd Co R.E. Billets from 98th Fd Co R.E.	
H.36.c.3.7.	12th		Worked on tracks through GLENCORSE WOOD and NONNE BOSCHEN. Moved camp to ELZENWALLE CHATEAU (H.36.c.3.7)	

Army Form C. 2118.

WAR DIARY
or
INTELLIGENCE SUMMARY.
(Erase heading not required.)

Instructions regarding War Diaries and Intelligence Summaries are contained in F. S. Regs., Part II. and the Staff Manual respectively. Title pages will be prepared in manuscript.

Place	Date	Hour	Summary of Events and Information	Remarks and references to Appendices
ELZENWALLE	13th		Worked as yesterday	
CHATEAU	14th		ditto	
H.36.c.3.7	15th		One worked in camp. Also on track through POLYGON WOOD. Three sections worked on	
(Sheet 28)			ditto Commenced work in alternative track through SLEM	
	16		WOOD and MOANE BOSCHEN.	
	17		ditto. Two Casualties 1 N.C.O. + 1 O.R.	
	18		ditto	
	19		ditto	
	20th		ditto	
	21st		ditto. The Company handed over work to 97th Company R.E. Completed alternative track.	
MONT des	22nd		The Company moved to STUTTGART Q.24.d.8.8	
CATS	23rd		Worked on Strutting at 23rd Div Lines R.27.a.38. Lieut Wilson R.E. rejd on leave.	
27.Q.24.d.8.8				
	24th		The Company worked as yesterday also on Road at R.27.a.3.B. Lieut Cotta R.E. attached with 2 O.R. R.23rd Div. Fld. Coy.	
	25th		The Company worked as yesterday.	
	26th		ditto	

WAR DIARY
or
INTELLIGENCE SUMMARY.

(Erase heading not required.)

Army Form C. 2118.

Place	Date	Hour	Summary of Events and Information	Remarks and references to Appendices
Mons les Cats 27 Q24/88	Oct 27		The Company worked as yesterday. Lieut Cope R.E. went on leave	
	28		Worked as yesterday. Received wire instructing that all Ranks on leave before return should report to have their N3 [Warning Orders?] under instructions from Embarkation Officer Boulogne	
	29		Ceased to work under C.R.E. Xth Corps Troops	
	30		The Company worked a cleaning [up?] equipment etc in prep-	
	31		preparation for a move at short notice. All adjustments in kit & tools etc were made up as far as possible	

Whitby Major R.E.
O.C. 128 Fld Coy

128TH FIELD COY. ROYAL ENGINEERS
128TH FIELD COY. ROYAL ENGINEERS

121/7517

23rd Hussain

128th F.C.R.K.
Vol I
Sup1 & Oct 15
Jan 19

www.ingramcontent.com/pod-product-compliance
Lightning Source LLC
Chambersburg PA
CBHW081531160426
43191CB00011B/1732